ACADEMIC MOTIVATION SCREEN

Student _____ Date of screen _____

Date of birth _____ Screener _____

Circle the number in the column that best describes how you acted and felt about your schoolwork **this past week.** Tell whether you felt or acted in the way described **never, some of the time, a lot of the time,** or **all or almost all the time.** Be sure to circle the number that is under the column heading that fits your answer.

Questions

When you were doing your schoolwork
this past week, as best you can tell, did you:

	Never	Some of the time	A lot of the time	All or almost all the time
1. try your best to finish your schoolwork?	0	1	2	3
2. worry that others would make fun of how you were doing?	3	2	1	0
3. pay attention?	0	1	2	3
4. ask for help when you needed it?	0	1	2	3
5. care how well you did?	0	1	2	3
6. feel sad because you thought you would do badly?	3	2	1	0
7. give up when you got "stuck"?	3	2	1	0
8. fight "discouraging" thoughts?	0	1	2	3
9. keep track of what you completed?	0	1	2	3
10. plan ahead of time what you needed to do?	0	1	2	3
11. worry that you were not doing as well as other students?	3	2	1	0
12. notice that you were making progress?	0	1	2	3
13. put off doing your schoolwork?	3	2	1	0
14. set a goal that you thought you could accomplish if you tried?	0	1	2	3
15. figure out a way to be less nervous while doing the work?	0	1	2	3

SUBTOTALS ____ + ____ + ____ + ____

TOTAL SCORE ____

Erratum

The Academic Motivation Screen on the reverse is intended to replace
the original, printed on page 111. This new page provides a correction
for question 12, ". . . notice that you were making progress?"
The original page did not include the rating scale for that question.

Enhancing Academic Motivation

An Intervention Program for Young Adolescents

Norman Brier

Research Press
2612 North Mattis Avenue
Champaign, Illinois 61822
[800] 519-2707
www.researchpress.com

Composition by Jeff Helgesen
Cover design by Linda Brown, Positive I.D. Graphic Design
Printed by McNaughton & Gunn

ISBN-13: 978–0–87822–560–6
ISBN-10: 0–87822–560–9
Library of Congress Control Number 2005909586

To my wife, Shelley, my daughters — Elisa, Jennifer, Michelle, and Suzanne —
and my grandchildren — Naomi, Amanda, and Brady

Contents

Acknowledgments

I would like to express my gratitude to my colleagues at Albert Einstein College of Medicine, Alec Cecil and Jane Farcas, for their helpful feedback and suggestions, and to Lillian Martinez, for her secretarial assistance.

CHAPTER 1

Introduction

The Latin root of motivation is *movere,* which is defined as "to move." When motivated, youngsters engage in a sequential series of steps. They experience an urge to act; choose to respond to that urge by engaging in the activity; and, once engaged, put forth a high level of effort, sustaining that effort until the activity is completed. When motivation is applied in academic performance, youngsters eagerly desire to acquire school-related knowledge, willingly approach and engage in learning tasks, and exert effort and persistence while learning—even when experiencing such negative feelings as frustration and anxiety. Historically, classroom teachers have been expected to motivate students to want to learn, to display curiosity, and to persist at learning tasks. Teachers have been taught to accomplish this task by conveying warmth, providing noncontingent support, employing effective classroom organization practices, and encouraging student autonomy (Eccles, Wigfield, & Schiefele, 1998; Stipek, 1996). More recently, teachers have been encouraged to facilitate motivation by deemphasizing social comparisons and public feedback (Ames & Archer, 1988; MacIver, Reuman, & Main, 1995), helping youngsters to set goals and define strategies, and providing corrective and evaluative feedback (Schunk, 1983).

Motivation is especially problematic for youngsters with a history of chronic school failure, given their tendency to feel frustrated when doing schoolwork and to anticipate failure. They tend to avoid academic challenges, fail to become engaged when given a learning task, and exert low levels of effort and perseverance when carrying out learning tasks, especially if they experience frustration while performing the tasks. Responses to the questions Do I want to do this academic task? Can I do it? and What do I have to do to succeed at it? are usually negative. Youngsters with histories of school failure tend to view schoolwork as undesirable and often deny, minimize, or fail to see positive reasons for learning in school. They tend to expect to fail even if they do try; often attribute their failure to stable, internal causes, such as low intelligence; and feel they have little control over school outcomes and little ability to figure out what they can and cannot do to improve. In addition, they tend to have difficulty developing clear goals and standards for success, are often unable to regulate their attention and mood adequately, lack effective study skills, and avoid asking for help.

The program presented in this book employs a structured intervention format to help educators, clinicians, and parents increase the likelihood of youngsters' achieving academic success by addressing the attitudes and behaviors associated with improved academic motivation. In brief, the program enhances youngsters' desire to learn and to put forth, direct, and sustain effort.

Although the sessions in this book are aimed especially at youth at the middle school level who have performed consistently below grade expectations in reading, math, or written expression for at least one year, they are likely to be beneficial to the school population as a whole. The sessions are intended for in-class use. However, they can be adapted easily for small-group or individual use by mental health professionals. When the interventions are used in a small-group format, the optimum group size is six to eight youngsters.

GOALS OF THE INTERVENTION

The goals of the intervention are, specifically, as follows:

+ To increase students' willingness to approach learning tasks

+ To bring about a higher level of engagement while learning

+ To induce youngsters to demonstrate a higher level of effort

+ To help them persist at learning tasks, even in the face of frustration

The intervention consists of 16 one-hour sessions. Typically, these are conducted over an eight-week period. If required, the intervention can easily be molded to fit the specific needs and time requirements of a particular setting. For example, depending on the circumstances—including the unique needs of your class or group—the sessions can be shortened, divided, or conducted over a longer period of time.

BEFORE THE SESSIONS BEGIN

Prior to the first session, it is helpful to schedule a one-on-one meeting with each student to explain the nature and purpose of the intervention and to determine the quality and degree of that student's motivation. This process is guided by the Pregroup Student Assessment Outline, which appears as Appendix A. Another purpose of the meeting is to obtain a baseline measure of the student's motivation by using the Academic Motivation Screen (AMS), given as Appendix B. Alternatively, you may administer the AMS at the first session.

At this time—or at the first session—each student should receive a folder to keep throughout the sessions. Students should use their folders to store all the session handouts and related materials. By keeping their work organized, students can check at any time during the intervention to see what they have already accomplished and gauge their progress by looking back at how they did in past sessions. If you wish, you can encourage students to draw a design on their folders that they feel will inspire them to do their best.

SESSION COMPONENTS AND FINAL PREPARATION

Each session has five components:

1. Objectives, which state the specific purposes of the session

2. A knowledge base, which provides background information to help you present the session material effectively

3. A materials list, which notes the forms and materials you will need during the session

4. Leader guidelines, which help you sequence and structure the information

5. A leader review checklist, which enables you to keep track of the elements of the session that were adequately presented and those that need additional discussion or that were not completely addressed.

The leader guidelines suggest ways to present the material that are generally effective. You are encouraged to apply the guidelines flexibly to best match the particular makeup of your class or group. Therefore, before leading each session, review its objectives, knowledge base, and leader guidelines, and consider whether any modifications are required to fit the unique needs and characteristics of your group. For interested readers, chapter 3 provides an expanded knowledge base, describing in depth the literature used to develop the intervention.

The materials list for each session includes the names of any handouts or other items required. The handouts are grouped together in Appendix C and may be adapted and photocopied as needed. In addition to these handouts, you will need ordinary school supplies that are generally available—such as a chalkboard and chalk, an easel pad and markers, paper and pencils, and so on.

YOUR JOB AS SESSION LEADER

Interventions are based on a student-centered model of learning. Students are encouraged to be the main speakers, whereas you—as the leader—are viewed primarily as a facilitator, who asks questions, rather than as an instructor, who gives the answers. In addition to raising questions and structuring sessions, as facilitator you stimulate student involvement; encourage the expression, elaboration, and clarification of ideas; highlight significant ideas during discussions; and stimulate and give feedback. Thus you should regard student participation as essential and treat it as praiseworthy. Whenever possible, encourage students to comment on the ideas that have been expressed by their peers.

KEY INSTRUCTIONAL METHODS

Storytelling, role-playing, and homework assignments are the three key instructional methods used in the sessions:

+ *Storytelling* facilitates student involvement and awareness by providing students with a fictional protagonist with whom they can identify and whose circumstances they can use to compare and clarify their own thoughts and feelings.

+ *Role-playing* is used to help students experience the feelings, thoughts, and actions they might experience when faced with actual situations that challenge their ability to demonstrate their level of motivation. Role plays allow them to practice employing alternative solutions to problem situations, act out motivation-facilitating behaviors, and have the opportunity to receive corrective and evaluative feedback. The role plays also provide modeling experiences for the students who observe them, giving them the opportunity to learn by imitation.

✦ *Homework assignments* are intended to increase students' focus on their own level of motivation and encourage them to try to transfer the ideas they learn in the class or group to real-life situations. In addition, by requesting that students track their efforts on a daily basis, you are helping them learn to be more aware of their level of motivation.

GAUGING HOW WELL THE INTERVENTION WORKS

The Academic Motivation Tracking Form, given in the first session as Handout 3, features an "effort thermometer" that youngsters use to measure their overall level of effort each day. One way of gauging the effectiveness of the sessions is to compare the average effort scores obtained during the first three sessions to the average effort scores obtained during the last three sessions. Another way of gauging the effectiveness of the intervention is to compare the initial Academic Motivation Screen score, obtained during the first session, with the final score, obtained at the last session.

PARENT INVOLVEMENT

If teachers are to be successful in enhancing students' motivation, it is important for parents and other caregivers to become partners in the effort. To be successful partners, parents need to demonstrate support for their children's schoolwork by becoming actively involved in their children's school experience and by exhibiting a positive attitude toward their children's school accomplishments.

The information presented in Appendix D is intended to elicit parents' support for the intervention and for the values promoted by the intervention sessions. The first item is a sample letter to parents or guardians describing the intervention and requesting permission for the child's participation. Session leaders may adapt this letter as needed. The second item is a handout titled "How Parents and Caregivers Influence Academic Motivation," a summary of the knowledge base that answers the questions that parents commonly have about how they can enhance their children's motivation to do the best they can on their schoolwork.

If resources permit, the information in the handout can be presented in a parent workshop. In the workshop, parents can read the handout and discuss the questions and answers with one another, while a workshop leader facilitates. Specific topics of discussion include what their children are likely to be thinking about when they try to do their schoolwork, how their own attitudes about school affect how much their children try, and how judging their children's schoolwork affects their children's motivation. If a second workshop is possible, parents can try out some of the ideas on the handout to help their children, then share their experiences when the group reconvenes.

CHAPTER 2

Intervention Sessions

SESSION 1

Objectives

- ✦ To clarify the principal purpose of the sessions, which is to increase students' motivation to do their best when doing schoolwork

- ✦ To increase students' understanding of the meaning of the term motivation

- ✦ To increase students' awareness of the following:

  Their level of motivation

  The value they attach to performing academic tasks well

  The importance of focusing on their effort and progress rather than how they are doing compared to others

Knowledge Base

Motivated students want to learn, try by putting out as much effort as they can, and maintain their effort even when frustrated or anxious. Youngsters are more likely to be motivated if they see schoolwork as important to them—that is, as valuable and attractive—and if they see that exerting effort at school is a way to achieve a goal or purpose that they feel matters to them. In addition, youngsters are more motivated when they are engaged in a school activity—involved and able to fully focus their attention. Last, students are more likely to be motivated when they want to learn in order to experience pride, become more competent, and judge how they are doing by the progress they are making. They are less motivated when they exert effort to please others, have others judge them favorably, or outperform others.

Materials

Copies of the Academic Motivation Screen (Appendix B; *optional*)

Copies of the What I Like to Do Most Inventory (Handout 1)

Feelings Faces (Handout 2), displayed in a whole-group format

Copies of the Academic Motivation Tracking Form (Handout 3)

Folders and colored markers

Leader Guidelines

Note: If the intervention is being carried out as a small group, outside of the classroom environment, introduce yourself and have students introduce themselves and ask each to state their understanding of the purpose of the group.

1. Tell students that the purpose of the sessions is to help them to try their best at their schoolwork. Explain that today the discussion will focus on how students can tell whether they are trying their best and why some students might want to try, whereas others might not. Also let them know that the group will discuss the difficulty in sustaining effort, even when students want very much to try.

2. If you have not already obtained students' responses during the one-on-one meeting prior to this session, distribute the copies of the Academic Motivation Screen and have students complete it. Let them know that their answers today will help you see how much the sessions help them. When they have finished, collect the form.

3. Ask students to think of something they like doing, such as playing a video game or participating in a sport, and to respond aloud to the following comments and questions:

   Name something you enjoy doing.

   Describe how you can tell when you are trying your best.

   What feels good about trying your best?

   What could happen that would cause you to give up or stop trying altogether?

   Ask the group to think of something they do not like doing, such as cleaning up their room or doing homework that is difficult and boring, and to respond as before:

   Name something you don't like doing.

   How can you tell when you're not trying your best?

   What, if anything, feels bad about not trying your best (for instance, having a parent punish you)?

   What could happen that might make you try harder?

4. Read the following two descriptions to the group. The first illustrates the attitudes and behaviors of John, a motivated

student; the second illustrates the attitudes and behaviors of Jane, an unmotivated student.

John

John likes being at school, especially on Wednesdays, when he has science class. His aunt got him a telescope that he uses every night to look at the stars, and he feels proud when his science teacher calls on him to talk about the solar system. John is also proud of how much more he knows now than he did at the beginning of the school year.

Jane

Jane hates Sunday nights. Sunday night comes right before Monday, the first of five boring school days till Saturday. She thinks school is a waste of time and finds nothing about school interesting or important to her. Jane sometimes puts some effort into her work when her mother promises to buy her something if she does OK. But most of the time, she notices that everyone seems to do better than she does at whatever the teacher is asking the class to do. When that happens, Jane begins to feel bored and then stops trying altogether.

5. Have the group discuss the two descriptions. Ask students whether they are more like John, the motivated student; Jane, the unmotivated student; or a combination of John and Jane. Have them explain the ways they think they are alike or different. Highlight in the discussion the degree to which students want to try to do a task and whether or how much they value effort, pride, perseverance, and making progress in small, steady steps toward a goal.

   Whenever possible, emphasize to students how rewards affect motivation. Ask students whether they think rewards for doing your best are good or not (that is, if "intrinsic motivation" is better than "extrinsic motivation"). Point out that parents or teachers won't always reward you for doing good schoolwork, but it's always possible to tell yourself you're doing a good job.

6. Distribute the What I Like to Do Most Inventory (Handout 1) and have students fill it out. Then ask them the following questions about each area:

   Do you usually try your best at these activities? How can you tell whether you are trying your best?

Are you more involved and focused when you try your best, or are you less involved and focused?

Which comes first—being involved or trying your best?

Do you try less when you know that you are not doing well, when you see that others are doing better, or when you are scared that you will be teased or criticized if you fail to do well?

7. Model a student's thinking aloud. Act as if you are initially motivated to do your best, then lose your motivation because you are not doing well and are scared of looking bad compared to others:

   (Walking to class) "My favorite time of day is 10:00. That's when I go to math class. I've been getting good grades in math, and I really like Ms. Johnson. I always feel really motivated—not just because of the good grades, but because I feel I really understand the work."

   (Sitting in class) "I see that today we're going to start working on number problems. I don't understand this. I looked ahead in my math book at some of those problems and I felt really dumb. What if I can't do any of them and everyone laughs at me."

8. Ask the students to brainstorm ways the student you portrayed could possibly regain motivation (for example, asking for help from friends, teachers, or parents). If students are unfamiliar with brainstorming, explain that it means thinking of as many ways as possible to deal with a situation without stopping to decide whether your ideas are good or bad. Using the Feelings Faces poster, ask students to pick the feelings they think they might have if they were in the situation you modeled.

9. After discussion, use as many of the brainstorming suggestions as possible and ask for volunteers to role-play the part of the student who started out motivated but then lost motivation. If not all students are familiar with role-playing, explain that it means acting out a situation as though you are the person or people in it.

10. After the role plays, model giving positive, specific feedback to the volunteers, both for participating and for exhibiting accurate portrayals of the brainstorming ideas offered by the group. Ask whether anyone in the group could say what the volunteers did well in portraying the suggestions and what

they might have done differently (as opposed to what they might have done wrong).

11. Give each student a copy of the Academic Tracking Form. Ask students to look at the effort thermometer (Item 1) and, with a check mark, indicate the location on the thermometer (from 0 to 100) that best indicates the effort they feel they put forth on their academic work during the last week. Ask for volunteers to tell the group their effort thermometer "readings." Briefly review other parts of the form and encourage students to fill out these parts.

12. Give each student a folder and explain that they will use it to save all the materials they receive during the sessions. Make the markers available and encourage students to create a design or illustration on the cover that they feel might inspire them to do their best.

13. Let students know that they will be given a new tracking form to fill out after each session and that they may be asked to read their completed forms aloud. Explain that the form is to be completed at the end of each session and then placed in the folder.

Note: Determine a central location for blank tracking forms and let students know they can pick them up freely, whenever they wish.

SESSION 1: LEADER REVIEW

Leader _____ **Date** _____

Indicate in the appropriate column which topics were adequately discussed in Session 1 (**A**), which topics need additional discussion (**B**), and which topics have not yet been discussed (**C**).

	A	B	C
1. The purpose of the intervention	❏	❏	❏
2. The meaning of the term *motivation*	❏	❏	❏
3. The importance of seeing schoolwork as attractive or valuable	❏	❏	❏
4. The importance of judging success according to effort, persistence, and incremental progress	❏	❏	❏
5. How comparisons to others, engagement, failure, and criticism affect motivation	❏	❏	❏
6. Identifying and expressing feelings associated with changes in motivation	❏	❏	❏
7. Using the Academic Motivation Tracking Form	❏	❏	❏

Comments

_____

_____

_____

_____

_____

SESSION 2

Objectives

+ To provide information about how the purpose students have for trying to do their schoolwork affects their motivation

+ To elicit students' beliefs, or interpretations, about the causes of poor achievement

+ To provide information about students' expectations for school success and how expectations affect motivation

+ To increase awareness of students' feelings about the adequacy of their school performance and their understanding of how these feelings affect motivation

Knowledge Base

The goals they have or the reasons students exert effort when doing schoolwork fall into two broad categories: Some students exert effort to experience pride and feelings of mastery. Others do so to elicit favorable judgments from others or to avoid negative judgments. Students who exert effort to experience pride and mastery tend to focus on how to do a task well and what they will learn by doing it. Students who exert effort to gain favorable judgments or avoid negative judgments tend to focus on looking or doing better than others. Students who focus on pride and mastery are usually able to maintain their motivation better than students who focus on how they are doing compared to others. In addition to the effects of goals on motivation, expectations about future success also affect motivation. Expectations about future success are based primarily on students' past school performance and their explanations or interpretations of the causes of past school difficulties. Motivation is higher when youngsters expect to be successful and believe that their poor achievement in the past is due to factors they can control or influence, such as lack of effort or poor use of learning strategies.

Materials

Students' completed Academic Motivation Tracking Forms

Feelings Faces display

Copies or whole-group display of Students Doing Schoolwork I (Handout 4)

Copies of Estimating Your Level of School Stress (Handout 5)

Chalkboard or easel pad

Leader Guidelines

1. Review the previous session, asking students to state the topics or ideas that they remember. After the students present their ideas, summarize any ideas they did not mention. Present any material from prior sessions that has not been completely addressed.

2. Review the students' completed Academic Motivation Tracking Forms. Ask for volunteers to present their forms and, individually, present each of the forms to the group. Have students start with an estimate of their effort to try their best. Praise the effort taken to complete the form and any indications of self-awareness demonstrated during the presentation.

    If a student has incorrectly completed a section of the form, use this situation as an opportunity to model how to give feedback: First provide positive feedback, then point out an alternative to any errors. Avoid making any critical comments. After you have modeled the procedure, ask students to provide feedback to one another. Restate the importance of giving positive feedback first, saying what someone could do differently rather than saying what they did wrong, and considering errors as opportunities to correct mistakes and improve.

3. Read the following descriptions of two students:

Eduardo

Eduardo wants to learn. He knows that to learn, he has to try hard. He listens carefully when the teacher speaks; he often raises his hand to ask and answer questions; and, at night, he likes to think about what new things he has learned during the day. He feels proud when he thinks that his hard work is the main reason he is getting good grades.

Felice

Felice achieves very poor grades on almost every test. She is very frightened of looking stupid and of being the dumbest student in her class. Because of her fear of looking dumb, she never raises her hand, stops working when other students glance at her work, and usually cannot concentrate because she keeps worrying about how bad she is at schoolwork compared to the other students.

4. Ask the students to brainstorm and state all the reasons they can think of to explain why Eduardo is very successful at his schoolwork and why Felice is very unsuccessful. Ask what seems to be important to Eduardo and Felice about either doing well or not doing well at school. In other words, ask what seem to be the main reasons that Eduardo tries to do well and Felice does not try to do well.

5. Divide the students' reasons for doing well or not well into two categories: reasons that describe an internal, fixed (uncontrollable) cause, such as not being smart, and reasons that describe an external cause that a student can do something about, such as trying harder. Introduce the following questions:

   Do you have to like schoolwork or see schoolwork as important to try hard?

   Do you need to believe that you can do the work?

   Is it important to compare how you are doing to how other students are doing?

   How can you tell if you did a good job: by your grades, by your effort, by the amount of personal progress you make, or by whether you did better or worse than others?

   Ask students to describe their own reasons for either trying their best or not trying their best at schoolwork and whether they can do something about their reasons if they want to.

6. Refer students to the Students Doing Schoolwork I pictures and to the Feelings Faces display. Ask them to identify the feeling that best matches the student in each picture. Encourage them to give examples of times they have experienced one of these feelings while doing schoolwork. Ask what feelings they have when they do well at schoolwork and what feelings they have when they do poorly.

7. Give each student a copy of the Estimating Your Level of School Stress handout. Ask each student to complete the form by estimating the level of stress he or she experiences when doing difficult schoolwork. Ask students whether anything helps reduce their level of stress and, if so, to describe what it is.

8. Remind students to pick up blank copies of the tracking form. Instruct them to fill these forms out, one per day, until the next session and to remember to bring these forms and their folders.

SESSION 2: LEADER REVIEW

Date of session _____

Indicate in the appropriate column which topics were adequately discussed **(A)**, which need additional discussion **(B)**, and which topics have not yet been addressed **(C)**.

	A	B	C
1. How goals affect motivation	❏	❏	❏
2. How beliefs about the causes of school failure affect motivation	❏	❏	❏
3. How expectations affect motivation	❏	❏	❏
4. How feelings affect motivation	❏	❏	❏

Comments

_____

_____

_____

_____

_____

SESSION 3

Objectives

+ To help students appreciate the effects of social comparisons and peer and parent feedback on motivation

+ To encourage a view of ability as changeable

+ To convey that ability can increase through effort, effective strategy use, and the assistance of helpers

Knowledge Base

Students often feel competitive and judge how they are doing relative to how others are doing. For students with a history of school failure, the tendency to compare oneself to others tends to lower motivation and self-esteem because comparisons invite the distraction of worrying whether they will do relatively well. Students' motivation is likely to be higher, on the other hand, if they judge how they are doing based on the effort they put forth or the degree of mastery they feel. The ability to shift from a social-comparison point of view to a self-focus point of view is difficult, in part because school practices tend to emphasize students' relative standing, and because parent and peer comments focus on standings relative to siblings and other students. Beliefs about ability and intelligence also make it difficult to challenge social comparisons. The more a student believes that school difficulties are a result of a permanent, internal negative characteristic—for example, that he or she is a "retard"—the more defeated the student will feel. This follows from the assumption that if a lack of ability is a part of who the student is, and therefore permanent, there is nothing that can be done about it. If students can replace this belief with the notion that they can compensate for differences in ability by increasing effort and seeking assistance, their motivation is likely to increase. Thus it is important that students see successful school performance as the product of a reciprocal relationship between effort and ability. Students who are less able can still be successful if they exert relatively more effort, ask for help, and use appropriate learning strategies.

Materials

Students' completed Academic Motivation Tracking Forms

Copies or whole-group display of Students Doing School-work II (Handout 6)

Feelings Faces display

Leader Guidelines

1. Review the previous session, asking students to remember the discussion and to state the topics or ideas that they recall. After the students present their ideas, introduce any ideas they did not mention. Present any material from previous sessions that has not yet been completely addressed.

2. Review students' tracking forms by asking for several volunteers to choose and present a form to the group. Model giving and eliciting feedback. Highlight the importance of students' trying to determine how much effort they put forth; the events that affect their level of motivation; and their thoughts, feelings, and actions at these times.

3. Read or tell the following story.

   Tom

   Tom really wanted to do well in social studies, but he kept getting one of the lowest grades in the class. His friends, on the other hand, got very good marks, and when they talked about their good marks, Tom would make excuses about having to go somewhere so his friends would not ask him what grade he had gotten. Even though he had studied a lot before the last two tests, he still did not get a passing grade, and he thought he would probably mess up again no matter how much he tried. He wondered why he could not do as well as his friends did at school, thinking there was probably something wrong with him.

4. Ask students to use the Feelings Faces display to identify the feelings that Tom seems to be experiencing. The following questions may help:

   Have any of you felt like Tom? If so, could you give an example of a time you compared yourself to others and felt upset?

   What advice would you give Tom to help him feel better?

   Is it honest to say to Tom that he can be more "intelligent"—that is, that there is nothing wrong with him and that he could do better? (For example, could he do better if he tried harder, asked for help, or learned new strategies?)

How should Tom judge how well he is doing? Should he compare himself to others, or should he tell how he is doing by the amount of improvement he makes?

5. Read or tell the following story.

Jasmine

Jasmine stood in the hall, trying to find her test score on the list on the wall with everyone else's test scores. Someone standing behind her said, "Hey, look how bad Jasmine did; she got the lowest grade of everyone." Jasmine's face began to feel hot. Instead of continuing to look for her test score, she kept her face turned so the person who made the comment could not see her and then walked away as quickly as she could. When she got to her class, she felt that everyone was staring at her. Mr. Jones, the teacher who gave the test, began the class by saying the names of the students who did well and telling the class that the names of these students would be displayed on an honor role in front of the classroom. When Jasmine came home, she tried to tell her mother what had happened, but as soon as her mother heard that she had done poorly again, she interrupted Jasmine and said, "What's wrong with you? Why can't you be like your brother? He always gets good grades."

6. Using the Feelings Faces display, retell the story, stopping at relevant points, and ask which face best fits how Jasmine feels at these points in the story. Highlight the link between the messages Jasmine has received, her feelings, and her actions. Ask for volunteers to describe what advice they might give Jasmine. When possible, emphasize the importance of effort, judging yourself based on the personal progress you make, and the importance of asking for help.

7. Develop a role play based on Jasmine's story. Continue the story, having a volunteer playing the part of Jasmine use the positive alternatives the students have suggested.

8. Ask for volunteers to share personal experiences that are somewhat like Jasmine's and tell what they felt, thought, and did at these times. Encourage the other students in the group to give each volunteer feedback on how he or she dealt with the situation, first saying what the student did well and then what the student might have done differently.

9. Ask students if they think that some people are born with a lot of school abilities and find school easy, whereas others are born with fewer school abilities and find school difficult. Have they ever tried to do something that at first they were very bad at but eventually got a lot better at? How do they think they eventually got a lot better? When possible, emphasize the role of effort, focusing on personal progress and the use of advisors or helpers.

10. Read or tell the following story.

   Mark

   Mark has always been told that he is slow. He is not sure what that means, but he does know it takes him more time to understand things he has been taught than it does other kids. Sometimes he forgets what he has learned and needs to have the same stuff repeated a lot of times. He usually feels too embarrassed to ask for help because he feels then everyone would know that he is not as smart as the other students. When his mother told him last week that he has to see a tutor, he felt mad that that she was making him go and scared that he would look dumb. To his surprise, the tutor was a nice guy. He showed Mark tricks to figure things out and remember things. Since then, Mark has noticed that he is getting a little bit better at some of his schoolwork. Mark is feeling proud of his progress and is beginning to put forth more effort. Now that he is doing better, he wonders if he is still "slow."

11. Ask students:

   What might the word slow *mean?*

   Do you think that Mark is or is not still slow, since he has improved?

   What did Mark do to improve?

12. Remind students to collect and fill out new tracking forms as homework and to bring the completed forms and their folders to the next session.

SESSION 3: LEADER REVIEW

Date of session _____

Indicate in the appropriate column which topics were adequately discussed **(A)**, which need additional discussion **(B)**, and which have not yet been addressed **(C)**.

	A	B	C
1. The effects of social comparisons on motivation	❏	❏	❏
2. The effects of peer and parent feedback on motivation	❏	❏	❏
3. The idea that ability can be affected by effort and by obtaining assistance	❏	❏	❏

Comments

_____

_____

_____

_____

_____

SESSION 4

Objectives

To increase awareness of the following:

✦ Personal beliefs about ability and intelligence

✦ How decisions or choices can influence school success

✦ Factors that affect positive and negative self-judgments about schoolwork

Knowledge Base

Students' self-perceptions with regard to intelligence and academic skills typically are based on their experience of how well or poorly they feel they are doing on academic and intellectual tasks and on the reflected appraisals of others, especially teachers and parents. These self-perceptions usually include "good-bad" judgments about how they are as students, as well as judgments about their capability to accomplish school-related goals if they wish. Motivation is higher when students believe that they have adequate academic ability, feel good about that ability, and believe they can control how well they will do on academic tasks. In these circumstances, students are more likely to feel able and confident, put forth effort, and persist. Motivation is lower when students believe they have inadequate ability, feel bad about that ability, and feel incapable of achieving success. In these circumstances, students are more likely to avoid academic tasks or give up easily. Thus motivation is enhanced when students feel that their actions play an instrumental role in achieving a desired academic goal. However, critical or shaming comments of parents, siblings, teachers, or peers are likely to decrease motivation. It is not the actual comments that affect motivation. Rather, the effect on motivation is based primarily on how the youngsters interpret these comments.

Materials

Students' completed Academic Motivation Tracking Forms

Leader Guidelines

1. Review the previous session by asking students to remember the topics and ideas that were discussed. Introduce ideas discussed but not mentioned by the students and then present

any material from the previous sessions that has not yet been fully addressed.

2. Review students' completed tracking forms. Ask for volunteers to choose and present a form and include whether they notice a change in their ratings on the "effort thermometer" (either up or down) and, if they do, why they think this is so.

3. Ask how students would define the words *intelligence, smart,* and *ability.* Emphasize the key elements in the definitions they offer. Compare the students' definitions with the following dictionary definitions:

Intelligence is defined as the ability to learn or understand.

Smart is defined as being mentally alert or knowledgeable.

Ability is defined as the competence or capacity to act.

4. Discuss how these words do not include comparison to others. Instead, the words share the idea that improvement is possible because everyone can increase their learning, level of alertness, and competence.

5. Read or tell the following story.

Jahna

Jahna sat in the dark in the room she shared with her cousin. She could remember the grades on her report card perfectly. It was easy; she had failed everything. Everything! Her aunt was going to say again what she had been saying more and more recently: "Maybe I should send you back to the group home. You are lazy and are going to wind up a loser like your mother." Jahna hated it when her aunt said these things. She didn't answer back, though, because she was scared that her aunt would really send her back. She wondered if her aunt was right. Was she a loser? She knew that since she had been taken from her mother's house and placed in the group home, she had been having trouble paying attention when her teachers were talking and felt too sleepy after school to do her homework. Before that, she had liked school, tried her best, and usually got good grades. She remembered a kid in the group home everyone made fun of and called retarded because he seemed so dumb. Was she dumb? Could she become smart again?

6. Ask students the following questions:

Do you think that Jahna is probably not intelligent? Is she mentally retarded?

Which facts does Jahna use to judge herself?

How are Jahna's report card and her aunt's words likely to make her feel?

What could she choose to do to see if she really is intelligent?

7. Ask whether any students have asked themselves the same kind of questions about their intelligence or ability as Jahna is asking. What did they do, if anything, to see how intelligent or capable they really are?

8. Using your own personal experience when you were roughly the same age as the students, model an individual's considering his or her own above average and below average abilities. For example, you might say:

   When I was 13, I was really good at sports, especially running. I was the fastest runner among my friends. I was also a great "fixer." When anything was broken around the house, I almost always could figure out a way to fix it, using my father's tools and his collection of screws and leftover parts. At school, I did about average in math but had a lot of trouble figuring out word problems and reading. It took me a long time to sound out words, so by the time I read them I forgot the main idea of what I was reading. I was also a terrible speller.

9. Encourage volunteers to tell about their strengths and weaknesses and to say how they judge whether they are either good or bad at something. Have any students improved in an area they were not so good at? How might they explain the reasons they have improved? Where appropriate, stress the role of effort, perseverance, and help seeking.

10. Ask students to check the Academic Motivation Tracking Forms they filled out since the last session to see whether they may have checked feeling scared that they might not be doing a good job on their schoolwork. Encourage students to be "detectives" in the future and to think of the type of schoolwork they are doing and what is going on to make them feel scared. Emphasize, when possible, the student's role in the situation (for example, didn't prepare, forgot to bring home a book).

11. As homework, ask students to be alert to situations in which they feel unsure that they will do well and, in the designated homework section at the end of the form, to write down some guesses as to why. Explain that students will use this part of the form when you give homework assignments for future sessions.

SESSION 4: LEADER REVIEW

Date of session _____

Indicate in the appropriate column which topics were adequately discussed **(A)**, which need additional discussion **(B)**, and which have not yet been addressed **(C)**.

	A	B	C
1. Students' beliefs about ability and intelligence	❏	❏	❏
2. The role of choice in doing well or poorly	❏	❏	❏
3. Factors that increase or decrease a student's academic self-esteem	❏	❏	❏

Comments

_____

_____

_____

_____

_____

SESSION 5

Objectives

✦ To encourage students' awareness of having negative and hurtful thoughts about the reasons for their academic difficulties

✦ To help students understand the importance of positive academic and intellectual self-perceptions

✦ To assist students in checking whether their self-judgments about academic competence are consistent with the actual information available

✦ To encourage students to develop positive and realistic academic aspirations

Knowledge Base

Sometimes students' academic self-judgments are based on the specific facts that they receive about their school performance; other times, their self-judgments are based on their erroneous interpretation of these facts. When inaccurate self-judgments are present, they often are a result of misinterpretations of social feedback or of the causes that underlie their school difficulties. Unless students learn to check to see whether their beliefs about their school performance are accurate, they are likely to develop a negative academic self-image and negative expectations about future academic success. They are also likely to undervalue their effort and personal progress and overvalue their academic standing compared to peers and the importance of attaining a relatively high grade. In forming fair academic expectations, students should consider the difficulty of an academic task relative to their own current level of academic strength and weakness.

Materials

Students' completed Academic Motivation Tracking Forms

Feelings Faces display

Leader Guidelines

1. Review the previous session. Ask students to state the topics and ideas that they remember from the last session, and then remind them of any important ideas that they did not mention.

Discuss any material from previous sessions that has not yet been fully addressed.

2. Ask for volunteers to present a tracking form. Where possible, highlight any increases in effort or self-awareness. Next review the homework. Ask for individual volunteers to tell about an occasion in which they were worried that they were not doing well on a school task; what they felt, thought, and did at this time; and what they thought was making them lose their confidence. Ask volunteers to imagine that they could take a time machine back to before this school situation occurred. Would they now do something differently (for example, ask for help, not give up so quickly)?

   Ask the other students to give the individual volunteers feedback, first pointing out what the volunteers did that was positive. If students do not offer feedback, model providing positive feedback yourself. Be specific and authentic. Explain that telling a person what else they might have done, as specifically as possible, is much more helpful than saying, "You did that wrong or badly." Now ask the students to tell the volunteers what they might have done differently.

3. Tell the following story.

Shawn

It was Monday morning. Shawn looked at his assignment sheet to see what he had to prepare for in the upcoming week. He saw that on Friday he had another science test. This would be the third test so far this year, and up to now, even though he had tried the best he could, he had never gotten a grade higher than 70. He decided to really, really try this time. He would study for at least one hour every night and participate in class more. However, when he tried during the week to ask Ms. Stevens, the teacher, a question, she never called on him. Shawn didn't think Ms. Stevens liked him. Several times, he was close to forgetting about trying, but then he decided to keep at it. Finally, it was test time. Shawn felt nervous. When he finished the test, he thought he might have done better than on the other tests but wasn't really sure. After his last class, as he was leaving the building, he met Ms. Stevens. She said, "I graded your test. Who helped you? You got an 80." As she walked away, she added, "I was surprised when I saw your grade." Shawn felt angry, wondering why his getting a better grade was such a surprise to Ms. Stevens and why she would think he could not do well on his own. Shawn's best friend, John, walked over and asked what Ms. Stevens had said. When Shawn told him that she said he had gotten an 80 on the test, John looked surprised and said, "You—how did you do it?" Instead of feeling happy and proud that he had accomplished his goal, Shawn felt upset, thinking that everyone expected him to do badly and that no one seemed to think he could do well.

4. Ask the following questions:

   Did Shawn interpret Ms. Stevens's and John's words correctly?

   Did his belief that Ms. Stevens might not like him affect how he heard her words?

   Could her and John's words have other meanings than the meaning Shawn attached to them?(Encourage students to give as many possible meanings as they can.)

   Is the meaning that Shawn chose the most likely meaning?

   What might Ms. Stevens and John have said that would have helped Shawn feel proud of his accomplishment?

   Let students know that when they hear comments from others about their school performance, it is important to be aware of what they expect to hear, to check out all the possible meanings of someone's words, and to take time to choose which meaning seems to fit best.

5. Ask whether anyone has had an experience somewhat like Shawn's. If students volunteer, ask them to describe their experiences. As a group, identify the key elements. For instance, in Shawn's case, some key elements are as follows:

   ✦ Trying but not doing well

   ✦ Trying but not having his effort noticed

   ✦ A teacher's having low expectations and not giving him credit when he did well

   ✦ Being upset by others' reactions and not being able to be proud of his accomplishment

   Role-play Shawn's and/or the students' stories, listing the key points to be included before the start of the role-play.

6. Ask group members to imagine themselves as the best learner they could be:

If this actually came true, what good things would happen?

What would you actually need to do, and not do, to be the best learner you could be?

Would you really want to do these things?

Do you feel that you are actually capable of doing them?

7. As homework, ask students to complete a new tracking form. In addition, ask them to do the following:

   ✦ Try to exert a higher level of effort than they demonstrated the week before, even if it is just slightly higher, and see whether they can maintain this higher level of effort until the next session. Ask them to choose that level now and indicate on the tracking form where it is on the effort thermometer. Each day, they can see how close they came to reaching or surpassing that point. If they do reach or surpass the level of effort they chose, ask them to see whether they feel proud of this accomplishment.

   ✦ Make sure students note on the tracking form any times during the week when they feel self-critical, ashamed, or embarrassed; what precipitated these feelings; and what they thought, experienced physiologically (their "body signals"), and did at these times.

SESSION 5: LEADER REVIEW

Date of session _____

Indicate in the appropriate column which topics were adequately discussed **(A)**, which need additional discussion **(B)**, and which have not yet been addressed **(C)**.

	A	B	C
1. The importance of identifying negative, hurtful beliefs about school performance	❏	❏	❏
2. The importance of identifying positive academic and intellectual accomplishments.	❏	❏	❏
3. The importance of checking to see if self-judgments are consistent with the facts	❏	❏	❏
4. Practicing setting positive academic aspirations	❏	❏	❏

Comments

_____

_____

_____

_____

_____

SESSION 6

Objectives

- ✦ To encourage students to recognize when feelings of helplessness are present

- ✦ To promote awareness of how one's actions and choices can lessen feelings of helplessness

Knowledge Base

Motivation is strongly affected by the degree to which students feel they can influence or control how well they do at school. Children and adolescents who have repeatedly done poorly at school tend to feel that their choices and actions have little or no effect on their school performance. As a result, they often feel hopeless and helpless in regard to improving their schoolwork. These feelings of hopelessness and helplessness typically are also associated with a belief that their school difficulties are permanent, global, and internal. As a result, these youngsters tend to exert little effort; avoid performing challenging academic tasks; act passively and nonassertively when at school; ignore information about their abilities that is hopeful or encouraging; do not ask for help; and give up easily. In addition, they tend to feel sad and have low self-esteem. To challenge these feelings of hopelessness and helplessness and change the maladaptive actions associated with these feelings, youngsters need to learn how to recognize their negative, self-defeating causal explanations about their school performance and substitute alternative, positive beliefs—in particular, beliefs that highlight their role in influencing school outcomes. Toward this end, they need to learn how to set short-term, realistic goals that are challenging but attainable and that are primarily achievable as a result of increased effort.

Materials

Students' completed Academic Motivation Tracking Forms

Leader Guidelines

1. Review the previous session. Ask students to think back and state as many of the topics and ideas as they can. Remind them of any ideas that they do not mention and present any material from prior sessions that has not been completely addressed.

2. Ask for volunteers to present a tracking form, and afterwards, to describe what they feel they have done well and what they feel they could have done differently. Ask the other students to give feedback, making sure that they keep to the sequence of first saying what the volunteer has done well and then stating what the volunteer might have done differently.

3. Next review the two-part homework assignment. For the first part of the homework, ask for volunteers to describe how they did in trying to increase their level of effort since the last session. If they were successful, ask whether they felt proud of their accomplishment. If unsuccessful, ask if they had any guesses as to why they were unsuccessful. Invite the other students to offer guesses as well. For the second part of the homework, ask for volunteers to describe times that they felt self-critical, ashamed, or embarrassed; what triggered these feelings; and what signals they felt in their body.

4. Read or tell the following story.

Stephanie

Stephanie woke up later than usual. It was January first. She had been at a New Year's Eve party with a bunch of friends till well past midnight, waiting for the start of the New Year. As Stephanie lay in bed thinking about the party, she pictured her friends telling each other their New Year's resolutions. She had listened, but because she did not know what to say, had not said anything. Thinking about it now, she thought that if she were to make a New Year's resolution, it would probably be about doing well at school. Yet she wasn't sure what she could really do differently so that she could do better. Up to now, nothing she had ever tried seemed to make any difference. Her grades were almost always just passing. The more she thought about how little she could do to get better grades, the sadder and more stuck she felt.

5. Ask for volunteers to explain what a New Year's resolution is. Using the ideas offered, when possible, explain that a New Year's resolution is a statement of what someone intends to do during the coming year. Ask why they think Stephanie was unable to make a New Year's resolution about doing well at school and why she seemed so helpless and hopeless about doing better.

6. Ask students whether they have ever made a resolution, or a promise to themselves, to accomplish a specific school goal:

If you did and were successful, what helped you to keep the promise to yourself?

If you did and were unsuccessful, what do you think was the reason for your lack of success?

Encourage students to describe occasions on which their thoughts and feelings about being successful with regard to schoolwork were similar to Stephanie's:

Why did you feel as defeated or discouraged as Stephanie?

What did you do or not do when you were feeling this way (for example, not try, put off doing difficult work)?

Highlight any commonalities that are present across examples.

7. Ask for volunteers to define the words *goal* and *short-term*, and the combination of these words, *short-term goal*. Using the answers offered as much as possible, emphasize that a *goal* is the end point toward which someone directs their efforts, *short-term* refers to something that will occur in the near future, and a *short-term goal* refers to something you want to have happen in the near future.

8. Ask for volunteers to pick a situation in which they felt the same way Stephanie did and to think of a short-term goal that they feel would be somewhat difficult, but that they could achieve if they increased their effort. If there are no volunteers, model the following example:

You have been frustrated in math class, and lately you no longer even bother to write down the homework assignment or bring the math book home. Now you decide to make a resolution to try to set the short-term goal of writing down what the homework is, bringing the book home, and working on the parts of the homework you are familiar with for at least ten minutes for the next three days.

9. As homework, ask students to complete their tracking forms and to note in the homework section any times that they felt helpless or discouraged (for instance, when asked to do math problems). Finally, instruct students to write down, for one of these occasions, a short-term goal that they are willing to try to achieve before the next session.

SESSION 6: LEADER REVIEW

Date of session _____

Indicate in the appropriate column which topics were adequately discussed **(A)**, which need additional discussion **(B)**, and which have not yet been addressed **(C)**.

	A	B	C
1. The meaning of helplessness	❑	❑	❑
2. How to recognize feelings, thoughts, and actions associated with the experience of helplessness in everyday school situations	❑	❑	❑
3. How to counter feelings of helplessness	❑	❑	❑

Comments

_____

_____

_____

_____

_____

SESSION 7

Objectives

+ To help students learn to challenge and reframe beliefs that contribute to feelings of helplessness

+ To encourage students to develop and use positive, alternative thoughts and behaviors when feeling helpless or hopeless

Knowledge Base

Once youngsters are aware of the negative thoughts that contribute to their feelings of helplessness and hopelessness about their schoolwork, they need to learn to challenge and replace these thoughts with alternative ones that are carefully selected to facilitate hope and a sense of control. Examples of negative thoughts and possible positive replacement thoughts include "There's no way I'm going to get a good grade," challenged and replaced with "I am going to focus on the amount of effort I put out" ; and "Everyone is doing better than I am," challenged and replaced with "I see the progress I am making." Problem solving can also challenge feelings of helplessness. When "stuck," students can feel empowered if they learn how to develop alternative strategies as a means of getting "unstuck."

Materials

Students' completed Academic Motivation Tracking Forms

Copies of Changing Negative Thoughts I (Handout 7)

Copies or whole-group displays of Changing Negative Thoughts II (Handout 8) and Problem-Solving Steps (Handout 9)

Copies of Estimating Your Level of School Stress (Handout 5)

Leader Guidelines

1. Review the previous session. Ask students to state the topics and ideas that they remember from the last session. Remind them of any ideas that were included in the session that they do not mention and present any material that has not been completely discussed.

2. Review the homework from the last session. Ask for volunteers to review a tracking form and say what they did well with

regard to trying and what they might have done differently. Elicit feedback. Highlight any progress made and praise any increases in effort and self-awareness.

3. Next ask for volunteers to describe a learning situation in which they felt hopeless or discouraged, the achievable short-term goal they set, and whether or not they achieved their goal. If volunteers were successful, ask what they did that led to success. If they were not, what could they have done differently? Ask other students to give opinions. Emphasize the role of effort and setting short-term, achievable goals and let students know it is important that they take credit for what they can do.

4. Ask students to complete the Changing Negative Thoughts I form. When they have finished, ask for volunteers to present their answers for each of the drawings. Afterwards, using the Changing Negative Thoughts II form, ask for volunteers to read each statement and propose a more positive, alternative thought.

5. Reread Stephanie's story, from Session 6, and ask for volunteers to try to substitute a more positive thought for each of Stephanie's negative thoughts. Whenever possible, point out the value of substituting thoughts about the importance of effort (and the negative effects of making comparisons to others) and of focusing on the relative progress that is being made (and the negative effects of defining success by a certain grade). Also point out, whenever possible, that when someone experiences difficulty, it is important to use problem solving to come up with alternative strategies for learning and for ways to keep trying.

6. Review the ideas presented in the Problem-Solving Steps form:

   ✦ **Step 1: Identify the problem.**

   Start by explaining the importance of defining the source of the problem, or reason for feeling helpless, in relation to a specific school task.

   ✦ **Step 2: Think of all the alternatives.**

   Review the idea of brainstorming alternatives—that is, spontaneously proposing as many ways of solving a problem as possible, without judging which ways of solving the problem are good or bad.

◆ **Step 3: Consider the consequences of each alternative.**

Once all the possible choices have been listed, discuss the importance of first visualizing what might happen, immediately and long-term, as a result of each choice.

◆ **Step 4: Choose the best alternative and try it.**

This step involves choosing a course of action based on a consideration of the consequences.

◆ **Step 5: Evaluate your choice.**

Stress the importance of self-evaluation: If the choice was a good one, pat yourself on the back. If not, try a different alternative.

7. Model having a school difficulty—for example, you always forget the definitions of words you learn in Spanish. Ask for volunteers to suggest alternative solutions. Once the list of alternatives has been developed, ask for volunteers to propose the good and bad consequences of each choice. List these as well. Once all the consequences have been noted, ask students to select the best choice; say why they think it is best; and explain how, after carrying out the plan, they can tell whether their choice actually worked. Emphasize the importance of noticing and taking credit for choices that result in improvement. Also emphasize the importance of changing a strategy if it is unsuccessful.

8. Conduct a role play of Stephanie's story, from Session 6. Ask for a volunteer to play Stephanie and, talking aloud, problem solve in order to get "unstuck." Tell the volunteer that if during the role play he or she becomes unsure of how to proceed, the volunteer can step out of the role and ask other students or you for help. Stop the role play when there are opportunities to provide corrective feedback. Afterwards, model and encourage positive feedback, noting what the volunteer has done well and then pointing out what the volunteer might have done differently.

9. In addition to completing their tracking sheets, instruct students to choose at least one occasion when they feel discouraged, then set a short-term goal, try it, and evaluate their progress in achieving it. Hand out copies of and review Estimating Your Level of School Stress, and then ask students to complete this form also, just before the next session.

10. Remind students to bring these two completed forms and their folders to the next session.

SESSION 7: LEADER REVIEW

Date of session _____

Indicate in the appropriate column which topics were adequately discussed **(A)**, which need additional discussion **(B)**, and which have not yet been addressed **(C)**.

	A	B	C
1. The importance of challenging and replacing negative beliefs and maladaptive actions when one feels helpless	❏	❏	❏
2. The need to focus on effort and relative progress	❏	❏	❏
3. The steps in problem solving	❏	❏	❏
4. The ability to apply problem solving in everyday situations when experiencing feelings of helplessness	❏	❏	❏
5. The importance of appreciating how one's choices can affect school outcomes	❏	❏	❏

Comments

_____

_____

_____

_____

_____

SESSION 8

Objectives

✦ To increase students' awareness of the presence of anxiety signals related to schoolwork

✦ To help students learn when and how to use relaxation techniques to combat school-related anxiety

Knowledge Base

Anxiety often undermines students' ability to maintain goal-directed behavior. In relation to school performance, anxiety typically involves excessive worries about the adequacy of one's performance and the possibility of failure on an upcoming school task, marked self-consciousness when doing schoolwork, and an overconcern as to how one is doing relative to others. Anxiety is usually manifested physiologically (for example, muscle tension), cognitively (for instance, worrying), and behaviorally (for example, nail biting). School performance usually declines when students are anxious because their anxiety and worries pull their attention away from school tasks and lessen their ability to absorb new knowledge. Training in the use of relaxation techniques provides students with a tool to combat anxiety. As part of this training, students learn to identify the body's reactions to tension and to use these reactions as cues to initiate a relaxation technique.

Materials

Students' completed Academic Motivation Tracking Forms

Feelings Faces display

Copies of Anxiety Signals (Handout 10)

Copies or whole-group display of the Rope Image (Handout 11)

Leader Guidelines

1. Review the previous session. Ask students to state the topics and ideas that they remember. Remind them of any ideas that were included in the session but not mentioned and present any material that has not been completely discussed.

2. Review the homework. Ask for volunteers to present a tracking form and say what they did well and what they might have

done differently. Elicit feedback. Highlight any progress made and praise any increases in effort and self-awareness. Next, with regard to the first part of the homework, ask for volunteers to tell about a time they felt discouraged, and the strategies they used to defeat these feelings. Elicit feedback and highlight what volunteers did well and what they might have done differently. When appropriate, highlight the following:

+ Replacing negative thoughts

+ Using problem solving

+ Being flexible

+ Setting short-term goals

+ Focusing on effort

For the second part of the homework, ask how many students checked four or more statements as true on the Estimate Your Level of School Stress form and what they think this finding suggests.

3. Read or tell the following story.

David

"Don't make excuses, David; I don't want to hear it. You better stop messing up and start getting good grades. I've had it with you!" David did not know what to say. He slowly walked away, thinking about how angry his mother was, how mean her voice sounded, and the big Spanish test coming up tomorrow. The more he kept thinking, the more he didn't feel right. His forehead felt tight, his hands were sweaty, and his muscles were kind of shaky. When he got back to his bedroom, he sat at his desk and picked up his textbook. He kept thinking that he was going to fail and that his mother was going to scream at him again. He tried to focus on the book and look at what he had to read, but he didn't even know where to start. The test was going to be on the last five lessons. He had read some of it but did not really remember what he had read. He wished he were like Jim, the kid who sat next to him in class. Jim always raised his hand and got good marks. David felt like a loser. There was no way he was going do well tomorrow and no way his mother was not going to scream at him again. As he thought about the test and his mother's screaming, David's head started to hurt more, and his heart was pounding. He put the book down, stood up, and began pacing back and forth.

4. Direct students' attention to the Feelings Faces and ask which word best fits how David is feeling in the story. Ask for volunteers to define the word *anxiety*. Using the students' definitions as much as possible, emphasize the following ideas:

   ✦ Anxiety is a nervous feeling that something bad is going to happen

   ✦ With regard to school performance, the bad thing often involves failing, being punished for doing badly, or embarrassment over bad grades.

   ✦ It is hard to do your best when you are anxious since anxious feelings make it hard to pay attention.

5. Ask students how David's anxiety is manifested through his body, thoughts, and actions (for example, his forehead felt tight, his hands were sweaty, and he kept thinking he would fail.) Next ask who has felt a little or a lot like David. Using the Anxiety Signals form, ask volunteers which anxiety signals they have felt most strongly in their own situation. If necessary, ask students what they felt nervous about—for example, were they worried about failing, being yelled at, being embarrassed, or doing less well than others?

6. Explain that signals of anxiety can be used as a cue to begin a relaxation technique. Furthermore, if students begin to use the technique close to the time that they first notice the reaction, the nervous feeling should not get too strong and they are likely to calm down more quickly.

7. Review the body reactions section of the Anxiety Signals form. Ask, by a show of hands, how many students have experienced each of the body reactions listed. For each reaction, ask for a volunteer to describe the specific location and the sensations that are present—for example, "My forehead gets warm in the area right above my eyes; it feels like someone is pressing on my head." Also ask students to state, based on a scale of 1 to 10, with 1 being the least and 10 the most, how intensely they felt the body reaction they are describing. Model the experience if there are an insufficient number of volunteers or key points are not raised.

8. Explain that a relaxation technique can help get rid of nervous feelings and that different people relax in different ways. Each student needs to learn which of the following techniques to be

demonstrated helps them relax the most. Explain and demonstrate each of the following techniques.

✦ **Muscle relaxation**

Focus on a few specific muscle groups, such as the hands, arms, stomach, and/or legs. Tense and relax a muscle, demonstrating how to focus attention on the sensations experienced during each phase. Especially illustrate the differences between the two phases. For example, you might make a fist and hold it in that position for about 15 seconds, then slowly spell out the word *T.E.N.S.E.* (saying one letter every two seconds). Then relax your hand quickly and slowly spell the word *R.E.L.A.X.* Tell students that while practicing, they should remind themselves aloud to concentrate and note the feelings of relaxation as they do.

✦ **Deep breathing**

Demonstrate taking deep, regular diaphragmatic breaths, differentiating between this type of breathing and "tense breathing." Explain that tense breathing tends to be quick, uneven, and hurried. Show how to take a deep breath through your nose, hold it, and then slowly and evenly exhale through your mouth. Model being natural and slowly filling your lungs with air and then slowly emptying your lungs.

✦ **Warmth/heaviness**

Explain that warmth and heaviness are sensations typically associated with relaxation. To illustrate this approach for students, imagine aloud that your hand is warm, as if in warm sand, in the sun, or in a warm bath. Alternatively, imagine that your hand is so heavy that it can't be lifted, as if a heavy object was resting on top of it. Another approach would be to imagine that a warm breeze is blowing lightly on your skin or that your skin is touching a warm, soft blanket. You can then model this technique in combination with muscle relaxation and/or deep breathing.

✦ **Guided imagery**

To show students this technique, imagine aloud being in a place where you have felt calm and happy. Note as many of the specific elements of the experience associated with a sense of calmness as possible. While doing so, include as many types of sensations as you can—specifically, what you heard, saw, smelled, touched, and tasted—in order to make the scene as vivid and real as possible. For example, you might describe a scene in which you are lying on sand and can feel the roughness of the sand against your skin or a scene in which you are smelling the saltwater and listening to the movements of the palm leaves.

✦ **Meditation**

Explain that in this technique, you calmly focus your attention and concentrate on a word (for instance, *one*), a sound (for example, *ohm*), or your breathing and, without force, try to maintain this focus exclusively. Explain that when your mind wanders, you gently bring your attention back to your breathing.

✦ **Counting**

Count backwards from 20, at a slow and even pace, simultaneously employing the deep breathing exercise. Explain that when students use the technique, they should count silently.

9. Ask for a volunteer to carry out each of the techniques that has been modeled. Provide feedback. Have the volunteers use the feedback to try again, when necessary. Ask for additional feedback, complimenting the effort shown and any relative progress made. If the final version of the demonstration still does not portray the technique adequately, model the correct version of the technique again.

10. Using the Rope Image, ask students to imagine themselves as a tightly stretched rope. Now ask them to choose and carry out a relaxation technique and see whether they can relax their muscles and loosen the rope. Ask for volunteers to describe how their attempts went.

11. Create a role play of David's story. Ask for a volunteer to create a way to use a relaxation technique in the role play. Ask the other students to give the volunteer feedback on when and how the volunteer applied the technique.

12. As homework, ask students to complete their tracking forms and, in the homework section, note a time that they usually

experience body reactions associated with anxiety. Ask that they try to imagine that they are scientists: They are to "experiment" and investigate which of the techniques that they have learned is most helpful in reducing their anxiety in this situation.

13. Remind students to bring their completed tracking forms and folders to the next session.

SESSION 8: LEADER REVIEW

Date of session _____

Indicate in the appropriate column which topics were adequately discussed **(A)**, which need additional discussion **(B)**, and which have not yet been addressed **(C)**.

	A	B	C
1. The meaning of anxiety and how it is manifested	❏	❏	❏
2. How to recognize and label body signals of anxiety	❏	❏	❏
3. How to select and correctly implement a relaxation technique	❏	❏	❏

Comments

_____

_____

_____

_____

_____

SESSION 9

Objectives

✦ To learn to use self-instruction to combat anxiety and worries related to schoolwork

Knowledge Base

Like relaxation techniques, self-instruction is a key modality used to combat anxiety. It is helpful for students to learn how to identify anxiety-provoking thoughts, challenge these thoughts, and substitute alternative, more realistic thoughts, especially thoughts that focus on effort and relative progress. A student's anxiety-producing thoughts related to school performance often concern anticipation of a negative outcome for a school task and worries that others will judge the student negatively while the student is presenting the schoolwork. Unrealistically high expectations often contribute to the student's anxiety and increase the chances of failing to meet those expectations. Thus it is important for students to consider their actual capacities when setting goals. In addition, it is important that the student define school success in terms of the amount of effort put forth or relative progress, not in terms of doing as well or better than others or attaining a specific grade.

Materials

Students' completed Academic Motivation Tracking Forms

Copies or whole-group displays of Changing Negative Thoughts II (Handout 8) and Talking Back to School Worries (Handout 12)

Copies of the Combating Worries Log (Handout 13)

Leader Guidelines

1. Review the last session. Ask students to state the topics and ideas they remember. Remind them of any ideas that were discussed but not mentioned. Present any ideas that have not been completely discussed.

2. Review the homework. Ask for volunteers to review a tracking form and say what they did well in regard to trying and what they might have done differently. Elicit feedback. Highlight any progress made and praise any increases in effort and self-

awareness. Next ask students to describe a time that they felt body signals of anxiety, then say what techniques they used to relax and whether the techniques were helpful in easing their tension.

3. Continue with David's story.

   As David paced back and forth, his mind kept jumping from one thought to another: about getting a failing grade and how, if he did, he would really look stupid; about the last time he got a failing grade and how all his classmates stared at him, probably thinking that he was a loser and that they didn't want to hang around with him anymore; and about how his teacher and parents will again be disappointed in him and criticize him for not trying.

4. Ask for volunteers to identify each of David's discouraging, negative thoughts. Using the Changing Negative Thoughts II form, explain and demonstrate that self-instruction can be useful in the following ways:

   ✦ Providing self-encouragement

   ✦ Directing attention toward relevant aspects of tasks (and away from irrelevant, distressing aspects)

   ✦ Challenging or blocking negative thoughts

   ✦ Monitoring and readjusting one's performance

   ✦ Providing positive self-evaluations

5. Ask for volunteers to propose alternative, positive thoughts for each of David's negative thoughts. Model these thoughts as needed—for example, you might say, with regard to David's negative thought that he is stupid if he gets a failing grade, that the grade is not the important thing. Rather, it is important to see if he put forth enough effort, and if he did and still did not do well, to figure out what help he needs to do better.

6. Continue to have students practice developing alternative thoughts, using the Talking Back to School Worries form. For each worry listed, ask for volunteers to propose various ways to talk back to the worry. After each proposed rebuttal, ask the other students to comment and suggest other rebuttals that could be used to talk back to the particular worry being discussed.

7. Ask students to remember any negative thoughts that they may have had in situations in which they were anxious about doing their schoolwork. Next ask them to picture a person they admire, or possibly a superhero, and imagine what that person might say to himself or herself in response to the anxiety-provoking event. Create role plays using some of these examples, emphasizing, where possible, the value of self-instruction as a way to provide encouragement and self-praise, a focus, a way to block unwanted thoughts, a means of monitoring progress, and a way to make self-corrections.

8. Review the Combating Worries Log. Ask students to fill out the log as homework, in addition to completing a new tracking form.

9. Remind students to bring these forms and their folders to the next session.

SESSION 9: LEADER REVIEW

Date of session _____

Indicate in the appropriate column which topics were adequately discussed **(A)**, which need additional discussion **(B)**, and which have not yet been addressed **(C)**.

	A	B	C
1. How to identify negative, anxiety-provoking thoughts	❑	❑	❑
2. How to develop alternative, positive thoughts to counter them	❑	❑	❑
3. How to use an alternative thought when experiencing a negative thought	❑	❑	❑

Comments

_____

_____

_____

_____

_____

SESSION 10

Objectives

✦ To help students learn to identify urges to avoid learning situations

✦ To encourage students to use self-instruction and problem solving to challenge avoidance and substitute "approach" behavior at these times

✦ To learn when, how, and whom to ask for help

Knowledge Base

Students who repeatedly fail at school tend to be highly self-conscious when engaged in academic tasks, anticipate failure, and, as a result, often try to avoid learning situations. They tend to feel that if they do try, they will experience shame and self-criticism because their schoolwork will not be as good as that of their peers; discomfort and frustration because they have to struggle to understand and retain the information that was taught; or embarrassed and humiliated when others notice that they are bad at schoolwork or not as good as other students. Avoidance can be overt (for example, being truant or skipping particular classes) or covert (for instance, faking an illness or delaying the start of schoolwork). In particular, students often avoid asking for help because of a fear that seeking assistance will demonstrate to others that they do not know how to do the work. To challenge and diminish the urge to avoid, youngsters need to do the following: be aware of their anxious feelings and their desire to evade a school situation; modify their expectations in regard to the threat of attempting to do their schoolwork, primarily by setting achievable expectations, defined in terms of effort and personal progress; using relaxation, self-instruction, and problem solving to diminish their anxiety; and try to approach school tasks.

Materials

Students' completed Academic Motivation Tracking Forms and Combating Worries Logs

Copies of the Asking for Help form (Handout 14) and the When I Want to Avoid Schoolwork Log (Handout 15)

Leader Guidelines

1. Review the previous session. Ask students to state the topics and ideas they remember from the last session. Remind them of ideas that were discussed but that they do not mention, and present any ideas that were not completely discussed.

2. Review the homework. Ask for volunteers to share a tracking form and say what they did well with regard to trying and what they might have done differently. Elicit feedback. Highlight any progress made and praise any increases in effort or self-awareness. Next ask for volunteers to describe their entries in the Combating School Worries Log. Ask the other students to provide feedback and brainstorm alternative solutions if any worries have not been successfully addressed. If there are too few "volunteered" responses, model potential coping self-statements yourself.

3. Continue David's story:

   David was tired of feeling scared. He was tired of getting criticized and tired of feeling embarrassed. So, on the day he was to take the next quiz, when his mother walked into his room to wake him up, he pretended his head and stomach hurt. His mother believed him, did not ask what was going to happen that day at school, and let him stay home. When he went back to school the following day, the teacher gave a quiz for the class to complete at home and said he would collect it the next day. David "forgot" to bring the quiz home, and when the teacher asked everyone to hand in the quiz, David told the teacher that he had forgotten to take the quiz home and therefore did not do it.

4. Ask for volunteers to say if they ever felt like David and to describe the "techniques" they have used to avoid doing their schoolwork. For each of the examples presented, ask what students predict would have happened if they had not avoided their schoolwork and instead had tried to do it. Elicit as much as possible the aspect of trying that the student saw as threatening, and determine whether the threat or fear was realistic.

5. Continue reading or telling David's story:

   David's teacher did not believe that he had forgotten the test and called his parents. David admitted to the teacher and his parents that he did not want to do the work because he was scared of failing. To his surprise, instead of yelling, they encouraged him to try his best and said that if he felt that he did not know how to do the work or was confused, he should ask them for help. David thought that sounded OK. He promised that he would try. However, the next day he did not understand what the teacher was saying. When he thought about raising his hand to ask a question, his heart started racing and his hands got all sweaty. He tried to figure out what he was scared of by imagining what he thought would happen if he did ask for help. He pictured the other kids teasing him for not understanding the work and then thought he would feel mad and sad. He remembered his promise to try, got up his courage, and, using the relaxation technique he had learned, tried to relax by counting backwards from 10, taking a deep breath as he said each number. He also decided to fight his fearful thoughts by focusing on how much effort he had made so far today and concentrating on whether he could do a little better today than he had been doing. Even though he still felt nervous, David raised his hand.

6. Ask for volunteers to say what they thought David did to fight his fear of trying (relaxation, revising expectations, reframing concerns). Next ask what the students thought that David had done well and what they thought he might have done differently.

7. Ask whether any students have ever wanted to ask for help as David did, but did not because, like David, they were too worried that they might make a mistake or feel embarrassed. Present the key elements of effective help seeking:

    ✦ Recognizing when you need help

    ✦ Deciding how to word your request

    ✦ Figuring out whom to ask

    ✦ Determining the best time to ask

8. Have students fill out the Asking for Help form, and then encourage volunteers to describe situations in which they asked for help. Have them include in their descriptions the person they asked for help, what they said and did when they asked, how they picked the time to ask, and how the situation went overall.

9. Have students create a role play based on David's story that includes the key elements of asking for help. After the role play,

ask students to provide feedback. Supplement the feedback, when necessary, to emphasize any of the key elements of help seeking that have not been mentioned.

10. Give students copies of the When I Want to Avoid Schoolwork Log, review its instructions, and answer any questions. Ask students to fill out this log as homework, in addition to completing their tracking forms.

11. Remind students to bring these forms and their folders to the next session.

SESSION 10: LEADER REVIEW

Date of session _____

Indicate in the appropriate column which topics were adequately discussed **(A)**, which need additional discussion **(B)**, and which have not yet been addressed **(C)**.

	A	B	C
1. How to recognize anxious feelings connected with the urge to avoid schoolwork	❏	❏	❏
2. How to apply the techniques of relaxation, self-instruction, and problem solving to challenge this urge	❏	❏	❏
3. How to learn effective ways of seeking assistance with schoolwork	❏	❏	❏

Comments

_____

_____

_____

_____

_____

SESSION 11

Objective

✦ To apply problem solving to counter feelings of anxiety and avoidance in learning situations

Knowledge Base

A problem-solving approach to lessening anxiety and urges to avoid schoolwork involves (a) getting youngsters to stop and consider what they are anxious about (for example, feeling ashamed or embarrassed, getting criticized, getting punished); (b) collecting facts and juxtaposing those facts against each fear to see if the fear is realistic or excessive; (c) brainstorming to develop as many alternatives as possible to cope with the fears (asking the question "What can I do to try?" to create a sense of empowerment); (d) checking out the pros and cons of each alternative by asking the question "What will happen that is good and bad if I make that choice?" (e) picking the alternative that seems best and having realistic expectations of success when trying the alternative; (f) rehearsing; (g) engaging in approach behavior; and, after trying the alternative, (h) evaluating how the attempt went and knowing that confronting a fear takes courage and is inherently successful and praiseworthy.

Materials

Students' completed Academic Motivation Tracking Forms

Whole-group display or copies of the Problem-Solving Steps (Handout 9)

Leader Guidelines

1. Review the previous session. Ask students to state the topics and ideas that they remember and remind them of ideas that were discussed but not mentioned. Present any ideas that were not completely discussed.

2. Review the homework. Ask for volunteers to review a tracking form and say what they did well in regard to trying and what they might have done differently. Recognize any progress made and praise any increases in effort or self-awareness. Next ask for volunteers to describe their entries in the When

I Want to Avoid Schoolwork Log. Elicit and supplement feedback, as necessary.

4. Read or tell the following story.

Sarah

Sarah didn't understand a lot of the work at her new school and was tired of feeling embarrassed. Yesterday, when she raised her hand to ask for help, her math teacher made her feel like a fool when he said, "Why don't you know that? Weren't you paying attention?" She decided she would start cutting that class—maybe just going for subway rides during school hours and not going to school at all.

5. Ask students to imagine that they are scientists who are pursuing information in a planned way, collecting facts by careful observation. In relation to the Sarah story, ask the scientists to hypothesize, or guess, in as much detail as possible what Sarah is feeling and thinking that is causing her to want to avoid doing her work. If there are no volunteers, propose that Sarah might be anxious at being criticized again or concerned that the teacher's comments might again make her feel embarrassed and ashamed. Ask the scientists to determine whether Sarah's fears seem realistic (based on the facts); brainstorm and consider all the possible alternatives that Sarah has to help her overcome her fears; consider what will happen, both good and bad, if she chooses each of the alternatives; and, afterward, explain how they could tell whether the suggestion worked.

6. Have the group create a role play in which a student is anxious about failing and is considering avoiding a school task by "forgetting" to bring home the work he or she needs to prepare. Encourage the students to refer to the Problem-Solving Steps and to role-play each of them:

   ✦ **Step 1:** Identify the problem. (In other words, why am I anxious?)

   ✦ **Step 2:** Think of all the alternatives. (What can I do to try, even though I feel scared? Can I do something I did in the past that has worked? Should I ask for help?)

   ✦ **Step 3:** Consider the consequences of each alternative. (What is good or bad about each alternative? What might go right? What might go wrong?)

- ✦ **Step 4:** Choose the best alternative and try it. (When I consider all the alternatives, which alternative should I pick?)

- ✦ **Step 5:** Evaluate your choice. (Is there anything I can do differently next time?)

7. After the role play, ask students to give feedback; supplement their feedback, if necessary, to highlight the importance of stopping and thinking about the problem before acting; considering other people's perspectives; separating facts from beliefs; developing more than one alternative; considering consequences; and, after trying the alternative chosen, evaluating whether it was a good one.

8. In addition to filling out the tracking form, ask students to use the homework area of the form to describe a time when they wanted to avoid doing their schoolwork and used problem solving.

9. Remind students to bring their completed tracking forms and folders to the next session.

SESSION 11: LEADER REVIEW

Date of session _____

Indicate in the appropriate column which topics were adequately discussed **(A)**, which need additional discussion **(B)**, and which have not yet been addressed **(C)**.

	A	B	C
1. How to appreciate the idea that anxious feelings are frequently associated with a desire to avoid school tasks	❏	❏	❏
2. How to see the desire to avoid school tasks as an indication to problem solve	❏	❏	❏
3. How to employ the problem-solving sequence	❏	❏	❏

Comments

_____

_____

_____

_____

_____

SESSION 12

Objective

✦ To assist students in effectively regulating attention, maintaining focus, and resisting distractions when doing schoolwork

Knowledge Base

The ability to regulate attention is a key requisite to maintaining motivation. In order to effectively regulate attention, students need to organize their study space; reduce or eliminate potential distractions; if possible, do their work when they are relatively rested and calm; create a routine or preplanned set of steps to follow; and, before starting, make a mental picture of the specific tasks that they need to do and the order in which they will do them. Once students start to work, they need to check, on a regular basis, to ensure that they are "on task." In addition, they need to use relaxation techniques if feelings of tension or frustration arise and become distracting.

Materials

Students' completed Academic Motivation Tracking Forms

Whole-group display or copies of Attention Helpers (Handout 16)

Leader Guidelines

1. Review the last session. Ask students to state the topics and ideas that they remember from that session. Remind them of any ideas they do not mention and present any ideas that have not been completely discussed.

2. Review the homework. Ask for volunteers to review a tracking form and say what they did well in regard to trying and what they might have done differently. Highlight progress made and praise any increases in effort or self-awareness. Next ask for volunteers to present their entries in using problem solving to deal with urges to avoid doing their schoolwork. Elicit and supplement feedback as necessary.

3. Read or tell the following story.

Alex

Alex had decided this marking period would be different. He felt he had enough confidence to try, even when he was nervous or frustrated. That evening, Alex intended to do his homework right after supper. When he sat down at his desk, he noticed that he had gotten an e-mail from Matt, his best friend, and decided to e-mail him back. Soon all his friends were instant messaging each other. Alex lost track of time. When he looked at the clock, he saw it was 9:30 p.m. He remembered his promise to try and went looking for his books. He looked all over but couldn't find them. He usually couldn't find anything in his room because it was a mess. Finally, under the pile of clothes he had left in the corner, he found the book he needed. Alex sat down again at his desk. He pushed all the stuff that was on top to the floor, turned on his radio to his favorite rap station, and, even though he was pretty tired, started looking at what he had to do. Instead of keeping the words in the book in his mind, however, his thoughts would jump around so that he would be thinking about something that had happened during the day or the words of the rap song that was playing. Alex began feeling more and more tired, tense, and frustrated. He decided that he would make tomorrow the day he really starts trying.

4. Ask the students if they ever felt like Alex. Ask what they did at these times to help keep their attention on their work. Incorporate student ideas whenever possible and present the following key points to keep in mind before starting a school task:

  ✦ Organize your work space.

  ✦ Pick a specific start time (if you are doing the work on your own).

  ✦ Create a routine or regular sequence of steps that you keep to as much as possible.

  ✦ Focus on exactly what you have to do.

  ✦ Make a plan as to what you will start with and what you will do next.

  ✦ Try to eliminate or reduce potential distractions.

  ✦ Use a relaxation technique if you feel tense or frustrated.

+ Keep checking to see if you are staying focused on what you have to do by repeating to yourself the main idea of what you have to do and making sure you are focused on that.

Key points to keep in mind after finishing schoolwork include the following:

+ Evaluate how well you paid attention.

+ Compliment yourself on any progress you have made.

+ Consider what you might do differently next time to improve your ability to concentrate.

5. Create a role play in which a student first plays Alex as he is described in the story. After the role play, ask students to look at the Attention Helpers and select ideas that Alex might use to improve his concentration. Ask for a student to redo the Alex story, incorporating as many of these ideas as possible. Give feedback, contrasting Alex's actions in the original role play with his actions in the second attempt.

6. As homework, in addition to filling out the tracking form, ask students to try to use the Attention Helpers on at least one occasion when they have to concentrate on schoolwork. After they do so, they should write down how the try worked.

7. Remind students to bring their tracking forms and folders to the next session.

SESSION 12: LEADER REVIEW

Date of session _____

Indicate in the appropriate column which topics were adequately discussed **(A)**, which need additional discussion **(B)**, and which have not yet been addressed **(C)**.

	A	B	C
1. How to plan when, where, and how a school task will be carried out	❏	❏	❏
2. How to employ the behaviors consistent with effective attention regulation	❏	❏	❏
3. How to self-monitor and use relaxation exercises	❏	❏	❏

Comments

_____

_____

_____

_____

_____

SESSION 13

Objectives

+ To learn to use study skills to maximize the benefits of high motivation

+ To incorporate study skills in everyday schoolwork situations

Knowledge Base: Sessions 13-15

Increases in motivation are unlikely to be sustained unless students acquire proficiency in such study skills as organizing their study space and materials; setting goals and schedules to attain these goals; managing time; and tracking goals in relation to time. Specifically, students are more likely to sustain their motivation if they are able to (a) create a study space in which distractions are reduced, items are arranged in an orderly manner, and needed materials are easily available; (b) break up assignments into their component parts; (c) arrange the component parts in a logical order; (d) develop a schedule to complete the parts in relation to the time available; and (e) develop a tracking system to assess their progress in completing the assignment, a system to periodically monitor whether they are on schedule, and a way to determine whether the schedule is working or needs to be modified.

Materials

Students' completed Academic Motivation Tracking Forms

Copies of the following:

+ Raymond's Disorganized Desk (Handout 17)

+ Where I Do My Schoolwork (Handout 18)

+ My Real Study Space (Handout 19)

+ My Ideal Study Space (Handout 20)

+ Assignment Sheet (Handout 21)

+ Assignment Planner (Handout 22)

Colored pencils or markers

It is often helpful to spread this session over two meetings, presenting the material on study space organization (Handouts 17–20) at one meeting and covering the Assignment Sheet and Assignment Planner (Handouts 21–22) at the other.

*From this session on, provide blank copies of the Assignment
Sheet and Assignment Planner in a central location, where
students can readily pick them up. If you wish, you can ask
students for feedback on the two handouts and then incorporate
their ideas in handouts especially tailored for your group.*

Leader Guidelines

1. Review the previous session. Ask students to state the topics
   and ideas that they remember, and remind them of any ideas
   that were discussed but that they do not mention. Present any
   ideas that were not completely discussed.

2. Review the homework. Ask for volunteers to share a tracking
   form and say what they will in terms of trying and what they
   might have done differently. Highlight any progress made
   and praise any increases in effort or self-awareness. Next ask
   for volunteers to describe the results of using the Attention
   Helpers to improve concentration. Ask them to say what they
   did well and what they think they could do better next time.
   Ask others to give feedback and supplement the feedback, as
   necessary.

3. Distribute copies of Raymond's Disorganized Desk. Ask
   students to follow the directions on the first page, circling the
   items that should not be there. When they have finished,
   briefly discuss.

4. Distribute copies of the Where I Do My Schoolwork and My
   Real Study Space handouts. First ask students to check off
   their answers to the questions on the first handout. Then refer
   them to the My Real Study Space handout and invite them to
   draw this space as it really is. They should depict the location
   of the study space in their home (their room, kitchen table, in
   front of the TV), including the furniture (desk, lamp, bookcase,
   etc.), tools (computer, calculator, etc.), and supplies (paper,
   pencils, etc.). After they have done so, have students share their
   drawings; highlight, whenever possible, the idea that being
   disorganized and messy makes it harder for them to study
   effectively and do their best.

   *It's OK for students to illustrate a disorganized and messy study
   space, if that's how their study space really is. Students enjoy
   drawing a mess—and it makes for a better contrast when you
   next ask them to show how they might make their own space
   neater and more organized.*

5. Next give students a copy of the My Ideal Study Space handout. Have them imagine an organized, neat, and properly located study space and ask them to draw its components on this handout. When students have finished, have them share their drawings. Again, stress the idea that their work will be easier and of better quality if their study space is neat, organized, and located in a quiet area.

6. Ask for volunteers to describe what they do when they get an assignment. Specifically, do they write down in detail what the assignment is or just try to remember what they have to do? Ask the students who write down their assignments where they write down the information and what they actually write, and then discuss what may be helpful in having a structured form to remember and organize important information about the assignment. Emphasize the idea that students are more likely to remember what they have to do and be more efficient if they see their assignments all together in one spot, especially if they include the times that the assignments are due. Give students a copy of the Assignment Sheet and explain that they will be using this form in the future.

7. Read or tell the following story:

Jane

Jane felt confused. The social studies assignment was so hard. She didn't know where to start. The teacher said that they had to do a research report on the president, telling about something that they thought the president had done that was good or something he had done that was bad. They then had to back up their opinion with information from three different sources: the newspaper, a book chapter, and a magazine article. They also had to take notes; make an outline; draft a report; and, after the teacher suggested corrections, write a final report. The teacher said that the final report was due in one month.

8. Ask students how they would do the following:

   ✦ Break up the assignment into parts

   ✦ Decide what they would do first, second, third, and so on

   ✦ Prepare a schedule to work on the assignment

   ✦ Create a tracking system to see if they are on schedule and to ensure that they are able to complete the assignment on time (by seeing how many days they have to work on the assignment and, based on the available time, figuring out the date by which each part will need to be done)

9. Distribute copies of the Assignment Planner. Review each of the sections and elicit suggestions for improving the form. Create a role play of Jane's situation. Ask for a volunteer to play the role of Jane and instruct the volunteer, as Jane, initially to act confused and then to use the ideas discussed to develop a plan to complete the assignment. Ask the volunteer to use the Assignment Sheet and Assignment Planner in the role play. Have the other students give the volunteer feedback and, as needed, supplement the feedback to clarify the importance of breaking up assignments, prioritizing tasks, developing a schedule, tracking, and monitoring progress in relation to the due date of an assignment.

10. As homework, in addition to completing the tracking form, ask students to pick the longest assignment that they have been given this year (even if they have already completed it) and create a plan for completing the assignment, using the Assignment Planner. As part of the homework, they will need to explain how they figured out how much time to spend on each part of the assignment to complete the assignment on time (counting from the due date backwards, periodically checking the time remaining).

11. Let students know that they should also begin using the Assignment Sheet to keep track of their assignments. Remind them to bring this and the other forms and their folders to the next session.

SESSION 13: LEADER REVIEW

Date of session _____

Indicate in the appropriate column which topics were adequately discussed **(A)**, which need additional discussion **(B)**, and which have not yet been addressed **(C)**.

	A	B	C
1. How to organize one's study space and regularly check to see that it remains organized	❑	❑	❑
2. How to break assignments into component parts and prioritize the parts	❑	❑	❑
3. How to develop a schedule for academic tasks, checking and tracking progress toward completion			

Comments

_____

_____

_____

_____

_____

SESSION 14

Objective

✦ To review and reinforce the effective application of study skills

Materials

Students' completed Academic Motivation Tracking Forms

Other completed forms: My Study Space and Assignment Planner

Copies of the Study Skills Checklist (Handout 23)

Leader Guidelines

1. Review the previous session. Ask for volunteers to name the study skills mentioned in the last session:

   ✦ Having an orderly and distraction-free study space with needed materials easily available

   ✦ Dividing assignments into logical segments

   ✦ Creating a schedule to manage the time available to complete the assignment

   ✦ Tracking progress

   ✦ Adjusting the schedule when necessary

   Remind the students of study skills you discussed but that they do not mention and present any study skills that were not completely discussed. Once all the study skills have been named, ask for volunteers to explain each skill. Provide corrective feedback as necessary.

2. Review the homework. Ask for volunteers to review a tracking form and say what they did well with regard to trying and what they might have done differently. Highlight any progress made and praise any increase in effort or self-awareness. Next ask for volunteers to use their completed Assignment Planners, first to describe the assignment they were given, and second to explain how they figured out how much time they needed to create the schedule.

3. Refer students to the My Study Space handout, which they completed during the last session. Ask students to say how many of the eight items they could say yes to, using the past

week as a basis. Ask whether any students have a number higher than the number that they gave earlier. If so, compliment any progress.

4. Ask students to describe a teacher they have had who made them feel upset by focusing on what they did wrong. (Be sure to let students know that they should not mention specific teachers by name but instead describe the teacher's *qualities*.) Create a role play in which one volunteer portrays this type of teacher and another volunteer portrays the student. In the role play, the "student" presents a completed Assignment Sheet and Assignment Planner aloud. The "teacher" responds in a negative, harsh manner, only pointing out the student's mistakes.

5. After this role play, invite the other students to provide corrective feedback to the volunteers. Supplement the feedback if necessary, emphasizing the ideas that a helpful teacher first tells students what they did right and then points out what they could do differently in a kind, helpful way.

6. Using different volunteers (and a different situation, if you wish), conduct a second role play in which the volunteer teacher provides a positive model, like the one the students just described, which does not hurt students' feelings but allows them to learn how to correct their mistakes. After this role play, ask students to discuss how they are likely to feel after each type of teacher's comments.

7. Distribute and review the Study Skills Checklist. For homework, ask students to use the checklist when they receive an assignment in any of their subjects, in addition to completing the tracking form.

SESSION 14: LEADER REVIEW

Date of session _____

Indicate in the appropriate column which topics were adequately discussed **(A)**, which need additional discussion **(B)**, and which have not yet been addressed **(C)**.

	A	B	C
1. The components of a good study study space	❏	❏	❏
2. How to figure out how much time is needed to complete an assignment	❏	❏	❏
3. How to distinguish between helpful and hurtful feedback	❏	❏	❏

Comments

_____

_____

_____

_____

_____

SESSION 15

Objectives

✦ To review the knowledge and skills taught in all the sessions

✦ To apply this knowledge to everyday situations

Materials

Students' completed Academic Motivation Tracking Forms and Study Skills Checklists

Copies or whole-class display of the Key Ideas list (Handout 24)

Leader Guidelines

1. Review the previous session. Ask students to state the topics and ideas that they remember. Remind them of any topics from the session that they do not mention and present any ideas that were not completely discussed.

2. Review the homework. Ask for a volunteer to describe the results of using the Study Skills Checklist after being given an assignment. Solicit feedback on what the students feel the volunteer did well. If the volunteer has checked no for any items on the Study Skills Checklist, ask what the volunteer thought was the obstacle that prevented him or her from carrying out the skill. Ask other students to brainstorm and propose ideas that the volunteer could use if these obstacles reoccur.

3. Let students know that there is one more session left. Explain that to be sure that the students get the most benefit out of the ideas that have been discussed in prior sessions, you are going to try to jog their memory. You are going to see how many of the ideas from the very first session up to now the students can remember. Ask for volunteers to state as many of the key ideas as they can. As students respond, check off the ideas mentioned on the Key Ideas list. After students have given all their suggestions, present any of the key ideas that they did not mention.

4. Give each student a Key Ideas list, and then ask for a volunteer to present a tracking form. Ask students to think about the volunteer's presentation and to say which key ideas the volunteer used. Next ask whether students can identify any key

ideas that the volunteer did not use but that might have been helpful had they been used.

5. Repeat the exercise with another volunteer, asking specifically for someone who can present a tracking form from a day when he or she felt unmotivated. Again, ask students to identify the key ideas used, if any, and to suggest ideas that were not used but that might have been helpful had the volunteer used them.

6. Tell students that there will be a party during the next and final session. Mention that each student will be receiving a certificate to honor the effort put forth during the sessions. Tell the students to be sure to bring the folders containing all of their tracking forms and other materials. These will be collected during the last session.

SESSION 15: LEADER REVIEW

Date of session _____

Indicate in the appropriate column which topics were adequately discussed **(A)**, which need additional discussion **(B)**, and which have not yet been addressed **(C)**.

	A	B	C
1. Review of the key ideas covered during the sessions	❏	❏	❏
2. How to apply the key ideas to students' everyday, personal situations	❏	❏	❏

Comments

_____

_____

_____

_____

_____

SESSION 16

Objective

✦ To celebrate completion of the training experience

Materials

Party supplies (snack foods, banners, balloons, and anything else that would add to the festivities)

Copies of the Certificate of Achievement (Handout 25)

Copies of the Academic Motivation Screen (Appendix B)

Leader Guidelines

1. Hand out the snacks and, while you do, reflect on the sessions. (Part of what you are doing here is modeling how to express feelings about ending the session.) Afterwards, invite each student to say how he or she feels and take a turn answering the following questions:

   Now that you have gone through these sessions, what do you think might be good or bad about trying at school?

   What are you doing "right" now about trying at school, as compared to before the sessions?

   What do you think you could still do better?

   Allow any students who wish to turn down this invitation to do so.

2. Ask for volunteers to predict what might make it hard to carry out some of the ideas that have been discussed during the sessions. Some questions to raise are as follows:

   What if peers tease you for trying harder?

   What if your parents notice that you are trying harder, expect more of you, and then criticize you for not meeting the higher expectation?

   What if a teacher or other school staff member does not see the improvement, continues to have a negative impression, or continues to criticize you?

   Ask the students to brainstorm possible alternatives to address each of the potential obstacles noted.

3. Have the students retake the Academic Motivation Screen, which they completed during Session 1. When they have finished, collect the forms and the students' folders, containing their completed tracking forms.

4. Distribute the snacks and the Certificates of Achievement. Suggest that students can use the certificates as a reminder to be proud of the effort they put forth and the personal progress they make.

SESSION 16: LEADER REVIEW

Date of session _____

Indicate in the appropriate column which topics were adequately discussed **(A)**, which need additional discussion **(B)**, and which have not yet been addressed **(C)**.

	A	B	C
1. What is good or bad about trying at school	❏	❏	❏
2. How to figure out what is now being done "right" and what could be done differently	❏	❏	❏
3. How to identify and solve problems when it is hard to maintain motivation	❏	❏	❏

Comments

_____

_____

_____

_____

_____

CHAPTER 3

Academic Motivation and Chronic School Failure: Expanded Knowledge Base

Current knowledge about the relationship between students' chronic school failure and academic motivation highlights three key questions that students typically ask themselves:

1. Do I want to do this academic task?

2. Can I do it?

3. What do I have to do to succeed at it?

Although these questions can be considered discretely, they clearly overlap. For example, high expectations for success strongly increase students' desire to engage in an academic task, whereas low expectations decrease their desire (Eccles et al., 1998).

The answer to the first question—Do I want to do this academic task?—depends on the degree to which youngsters see the school task as valuable, desirable, or attractive, as well as on the goals or purposes they have for doing the work. Youngsters can exert effort on an academic task, for example, either because they value doing well and like confirming that they are capable or because they expect to derive enjoyment or pragmatic benefits from working hard (Eccles-Parsons et al., 1983). Thus youngsters can be either *intrinsically motivated* and have a desire to carry out tasks for their own sake or *extrinsically motivated* and carry out tasks to achieve a tangible reward (Harter, 1981). A desire to carry out tasks for their own sake is likely to be especially strong when youngsters are fully engaged in the activity—that is, when they are able to direct and sustain their entire attention on the activity. This form of involvement, or immersion, has been labeled "flow" (Csikszentmihalyi, 1988); when it is present, students experience more pleasure doing the tasks and also place a higher value on performing them.

Different Goals, Different Effects on Motivation

Goals, in the context of academic motivation, relate to youngsters' reasons or purposes for doing their schoolwork. Goals generally are determined by youngsters' specific definitions of success or anticipated payoffs (Nicholls, 1979). Traditionally, students' goals have been classified as one of two types. The first type—*mastery goals*—is evident when youngsters want to perform an academic task for the purposes of learning, becoming more competent, and making progress. This type of goal almost always requires youngsters to put forth a great deal of effort. The second type—*performance goals*—is used when youngsters want to perform an academic task so that they can outperform others and maximize favorable evaluations of their work. Their standing compared to others' is central to their motivation, rather than the amount of effort they exert.

When school success is defined by the amount of effort exerted rather than by attaining a certain grade or surpassing others' grades, self-esteem is generally higher, and anxiety about school performance is generally lower (Pintrich & Schunk, 2002). Anxiety and negative judgments about schoolwork are less likely to occur because youngsters themselves can control and predict how much effort they will expend. They cannot control or predict how they will do compared to others.

How Students' Expectations and Levels of Motivation Are Formed

The second question regarding the relationship between chronic school failure and motivation—Can I do it?—is determined by students' expectations of the likelihood of their academic success and by their attributions, self-concept, and degree of self-efficacy. Expectations are predictions made on the basis of prior experiences with success and failure. Expectations strongly influence motivation: When youngsters expect to do well on academic tasks, their motivation is likely to be relatively high; when they expect to fail, their motivation is likely to be relatively low, especially if they feel their efforts will make no difference in preventing failure: When youngsters expect to fail and feel helpless to prevent failure, they are likely to become disengaged, give up easily, withdraw, and procrastinate or avoid doing schoolwork (Bandura, 1994; Urdan

& Midgley, 2001). At times, youngsters may avoid doing school-work to create the appearance that their failure is due to a lack of effort (generally, a less hurtful belief) and not to incompetence (generally, a more hurtful belief), which they fear would be demonstrated if they tried and failed.

Although students' expectations are commonly based on their subjective interpretations of why success or failure has occurred in the past, their expectations are not necessarily based on the actual, or objective, causes of success or failure (Weiner, 1986). For example, a boy who is unable to complete a math task may attribute his inability to finish the task to the noisy, distracting environment in which he was working, or he may see his difficulty as an indication that he is stupid. Interpretations of the causes of good or poor school performance can be sorted along two dimensions. The first dimension relates to whether the interpretation of the reason for success or failure is attached to an internal or external cause; the second dimension relates to whether the cause is stable or unstable—that is, something that is likely to change or something that is likely to remain the same. The more students interpret the cause of their school failure as internal and stable, the more hopeless, avoidant, and self-critical they are likely to be (Kirk & Chalfant, 1984).

The ability to make cause-and-effect determinations develops during elementary school. At the start of elementary school, youngsters often fail to appreciate how effort, ability, and performance influence and interact with each other. By about the third grade, youngsters begin to make distinctions between these terms and generally see school success as primarily a result of effort. By the end of elementary school, youngsters are usually able to distinguish the roles that effort and ability play in regard to school performance and can see that increased effort is a means of compensating for limitations in ability (Nicholls, Patashnick, & Mettetal, 1986). Around this time, youngsters' views of intelligence also become more diverse, with some children continuing to see intelligence as an invariant entity and other children beginning to see intelligence as a capacity that can change incrementally (Dweck & Elliot, 1983).

Self-Efficacy versus Learned Helplessness

Youngsters' beliefs about effort, ability, and intelligence strongly affect their motivation. Motivation is generally higher when youngsters believe they possess adequate ability; as a result, they can predict future success. Motivation is generally lower if youngsters believe they lack adequate ability; that is, assume that they have one or more "defects" that make it likely that they will fail in the future (Weiner, 1986). When youngsters do not believe that putting forth effort or trying hard will bring school success, they become less motivated; to regain their motivation, they need to see that they can do better with support and the use of effective, flexible strategies (Carr, Borkowski, & Maxwell, 1991).

A youngster's sense of efficacy—the degree to which a youngster feels that he or she can successfully influence or control the outcome of a school task—also greatly affects motivation. Thus motivation, measured by the level of the youngster's effort and persistence, is relatively high when the youngster's self-efficacy is relatively high (Bandura, 1994; Pintrich & Schunk, 2002). The concepts of "choice" and "volition" help explain the relationship between motivation and self-efficacy: The more strongly youngsters believe that their own actions are the primary determinants of a school outcome and that their actions are volitional or noncoerced, the more self-efficacious they will feel (deCharms, 1968).

The opposite of the feeling of self-efficacy is the feeling of learned helplessness. The latter involves a sense of defeat—a belief based on past learning that nothing a youngster can do will affect his or her ability to attain a desired outcome (Dweck & Goetz, 1978). This feeling is especially common for youngsters with a history of repeated academic failures; for these chronically failing students, learned helplessness often involves the belief that no amount of effort will result in academic success. Therefore, these youngsters tend either to avoid challenging academic tasks or to refuse doing them at all. As a result, they often try to protect their self-esteem by viewing their failure at school tasks as a consequence of a lack of effort and not as an indication of inadequacy (Covington, 1992). For these youngsters to continue to put forth a great deal of effort, increased support, including help in selecting alternative strategies, is usually needed to prevent or lessen feelings of learned helplessness (Borkowski & Thorpe, 1994).

Once youngsters decide to perform an academic task—and believe they can do it successfully—they need to focus on the third question, listed earlier: What do I have to do to succeed? Success is more likely if youngsters can regulate their behavior, employ effective study skills, and, in a timely and appropriate manner, ask for help. Self-regulation requires that youngsters be given opportunities to be self-reliant when performing academic tasks—specifically, opportunities to make and implement choices (Garcia, 1996). In turn, greater self-reliance tends to facilitate greater motivation, as indicated by a relative increase in the internalization of positive values present in the learning environment; increased curiosity; and a relative increase in the number of independent mastery attempts (Deci, Ryan, & Williams, 1996).

SETTING GOALS AND DEVELOPING STRATEGIES TO ACHIEVE THEM

Setting clear goals and standards helps students to facilitate increases in self-regulation. By forming well-defined criteria, youngsters are able to monitor continually how they are doing and to adjust their efforts and actions according to the affective reactions and self-judgments they experience (Bandura, 1994). Once they select their goals, they need to develop strategies to achieve them. Because chronically failing youngsters often have difficulty developing effective strategies, it is helpful to have them (a) observe a successful model implementing a strategy, (b) imitate the model, and (c) autonomously apply the model's strategy to a new situation, without the model present (Zimmerman, Bonner, & Kovach, 1996). Practicing self-observation is often necessary before youngsters can successfully evaluate their own progress. In addition, coaching is usually needed to help youngsters modulate their attention and deal with negative emotional states such as anxiety and dysphoria. Youngsters who are able to control their attention and negative emotional states are more successful academically than those who can't. They are better able both to focus on information that is relevant to attaining their goal and to resist distractions (Zimmerman, 1989).

Using study strategies such as acquiring, recording, organizing, synthesizing, and remembering academic information effectively is particularly important if youngsters are to feel successful (Gall, Gall, Jacobson, & Bullock, 1990). Planning is essential because success is more likely when youngsters prepare in advance. Youngsters need to select one or more strategies that seem best suited to them, to monitor and evaluate the effectiveness of these strategies, and to shift to one or more new strategies if the original strategies prove ineffective.

Typically, the first step in improving study skills is to examine the study space to make sure it is organized and as free of distraction and clutter as possible. According to Gall et al. (1990), the next step is to encourage youngsters to do the following:

1. Use a sheet to track and prioritize assignments

2. Break large assignments into smaller units

3. Note when and how long they will work on each unit

4. Organize their materials

5. Implement their work plan

6. Monitor, evaluate, and adjust the plan, as needed

Coaching youngsters to learn when to seek help is also critically important if they are to be successful at performing school tasks. Youngsters need to learn how to recognize occasions when they need assistance and use effective help-seeking behaviors on these occasions (Ryan, Stiller, & Lynch, 1994). Specifically, they need to figure out how to put their question into words, whom to ask for help, and the best time to ask. Youngsters with histories of academic failure are often especially averse to asking for help for fear that if they do, they will be judged negatively by peers. In particular, because they don't know how to do what their peers can do without assistance, they tend to be anxious that these peers will perceive their asking for help as proof that they are "dumb." Asking for help is especially hard if students feel socially incompetent and fear that they will ask for help in an awkward manner that only increases the likelihood of their being judged negatively by others (Ryan, Pintrich, & Midgley, 2001).

The actions of others also strongly affect the degree of motivation a youngster demonstrates. Examples of social influences that tend to decrease motivation include teachers' assigning schoolwork in a directive manner, allowing youngsters little choice in the process (for example, giving them no say in which part of the assignment to start with, failing to allow alternative ways of completing the assignment); parents' using threats to attain compliance; parents' and teachers' providing feedback in a shaming, demeaning manner (Ryan & Deci, 2000); and peer contacts' reinforcing a lack of interest in schoolwork (Berndt, Laychak, & Pack, 1990). Examples of social influences that tend to increase motivation include teachers' defining success in terms of effort and personal progress; parents' and teachers' deemphasizing grades and test scores; and teachers' framing mistakes as opportunities for feedback and not as prompts for criticism. It is not the parents' and teachers' actions, in and of themselves, that influence a youngster's motivation. Rather, it is the youngsters' perceptions and interpretations of these actions that are key (Eccles et al., 1998). For example, if a youngster perceives a teacher's positive feedback as critical, his or her motivation is likely to remain relatively low.

NEED FOR TEACHERS TO PROVIDE FEEDBACK
TO REINFORCE STUDENTS' EFFORTS

Early research examining teachers' influence on students' motivation focused on teachers' ability to provide positive social reinforcement (Dunkin & Biddle, 1974). Motivation was noted to be higher when teachers reinforced youngsters' effort at schoolwork with warmth and provided a supportive classroom environment (Eccles et al., 1998). Students generally rely on teachers' displays of emotion to judge how teachers feel about them overall and about their school performance, in particular. For example, if adults act angry, children as young as six tend to interpret the adults' anger as an indication that they have done something wrong; by about age nine, children tend to view an adult's show of sympathy, after they make an error, as an indication that the adult believes that the mistake was not their fault (Weiner, Graham, Stern, & Lawson, 1982). Youngsters' interpretation of adults' behavior strongly affects their confidence and motivation. Thus students are more likely to be motivated when they perceive that the teacher has formed a positive relationship with them; in addition, they are more likely to feel a sense of belonging when at school (Roeser, Midgley, & Urdan, 1996). On the other hand, students are likely to feel less motivated and more self-blaming when a teacher is angry, believing that they have done something wrong and have angered the teacher (Graham, 1990).

Steering Clear of Self-Fulfilling Prophecies

In addition to an emphasis on the effects of a teacher's personality on student motivation, research has also emphasized teacher expectations and values (Moos, 1979). When teachers expect that a student will do poorly, this negative expectation becomes a "self-fulfilling prophecy," and students' motivation lessens (Rosenthal, 1973). Furthermore, teachers tend to confirm negative, preexisting beliefs about students' capabilities and attitudes by selectively seeking information consistent with their beliefs, ignoring inconsistent information, or misperceiving student behavior so that it conforms to a preexisting expectation. In addition, self-fulfilling prophecies are reinforced by the increased likelihood that teachers will act differently toward youngsters on the basis of their expectations: They are more likely to be friendlier toward youngsters for whom they hold high expectations and to call on them more in class; they are also more likely to be critical of youngsters for whom they hold low expectations (Good, 1983).

How teachers define student success affects their expectations. In turn, teacher expectations strongly affect students' level of interest in schoolwork, willingness to independently master a learning task, and desire to maintain effort in the face of difficulty. For example, motivation tends to be relatively low, particularly for chronically failing youngsters, when teachers define success by comparing youngsters' relative academic standing or by the students' ability to exceed a uniform, absolute standard (MacIver, 1987). Motivation also tends to be relatively low when teachers convey to students that success is indicated by the ability group they are in or whether their names are present on an honor roll. Under these circumstances, youngsters who tend to be poor achievers often cease to try, feeling that no amount of effort on their part will guarantee success.

Motivation is relatively high when teachers define success as the degree of effort that youngsters exert—independent of the outcome attained—as well as the ability to improve from an initially low level of achievement to a higher level of achievement (Maehr & Midgley, 1996). Youngsters are more likely to feel that they can attain success when motivation is defined in these ways because the key requirement—effort—is under their control (Ames, 1992). Motivation is also likely to be relatively high when youngsters can contribute to the definition of school success because they are more likely to see success as personally meaningful. On the other hand, motivation is likely to be relatively low when the definition of school success is imposed. In this instance, they are less likely to feel that the reward, or payoff, that results from their efforts will result in something that they value or see as personally important—and tend to put forth effort only to avoid a negative consequence or to attain an external reward (Brophy, 1987). Relatively higher motivation is also associated with allowing youngsters to have input not only into the definition of school success, but also into other aspects of school instruction, such as which task they should start with and how long they need to work on a task before they take a break (Ryan & Deci, 2000). The higher levels of active engagement and feelings of control that youngsters experience when they are allowed to have input into school choices therefore seem to have a powerful influence in enhancing their motivation (Grolnick & Ryan, 1989).

Using students' effort to define success requires that teachers match the difficulty of an assigned task to a youngster's level of competence. Thus motivation is likely to be high if a task is challenging but doable, so that with sufficient effort, the youngster can attain success and feel proud of his or her accomplishment (Brophy, 1987). On the other hand, motivation is likely to be low if a task is either so easy that success can be achieved with little effort or so difficult that no matter how much effort the youngster expends, he or she will fail (Stipek, 1996).

The ways that teachers acknowledge and report success also affect youngsters' motivation. When teachers, in a highly public manner, emphasize who has been successful and who has been unsuccessful, motivation is likely to be low, especially for low-achieving youngsters (MacIver, 1987). Whole-group instruction, comments to the class that highlight who did well on a test and who did poorly, and displays in which the work of high-achieving students is used as a model for others magnify differences in students' abilities. This emphasis on the lower standing of students who are not as strong academically as their higher achieving peers increases the likelihood that the lower achieving students will withdraw or avoid academic challenges (Urdan & Midgley, 2001). Conversely, when teachers reward students for their effort and improvement, motivation tends to be higher because all youngsters feel capable of earning a reward. Motivation is also higher when students are encouraged to monitor and evaluate their own performance. Increased feelings of accountability facilitate an increased sense of control and autonomy, which in turn is associated with a youngster's attaching increased value to learning tasks (Eccles et al., 1991).

Why Positive Teacher Feedback Is Meaningful to Students

Teacher feedback is a critically important determinant of students' motivation. It is the primary means by which students can modify their performance, overcome obstacles to learning, and consequently improve. Motivation is higher when teachers provide accurate, detailed feedback that allows students to understand what they are able and not able to do and to determine when they need help. Motivation is also higher when teachers view mistakes as expected occurrences, particularly when someone is acquiring a new skill; when teachers act this way, they are also providing students with an opportunity to problem solve. As expected, motivation is lower when teachers criticize a student following a mistake, or when they shame a student. In these circumstances, students are likely to feel embarrassed and angry and to become avoidant (Pintrich & Schunk, 2002). Because students' motivation is primarily affected by what they hear, rather than by what teachers say, teachers need to check whether students heard their feedback accurately, and if not, correct any erroneous attributions. In addition, when giving feedback on students' failures, teachers need to avoid saying, in a rote manner, "You need to try harder," without first checking to see whether the youngster actually has or has not exerted effort. For youngsters prone to academic failure, a high level of effort is often insufficient; a change in strategy is usually needed as well (Carr et al., 1991).

Positive feedback from teachers is more likely to increase youngsters' motivation when the following holds true:

1. The link between the positive feedback and the task is relevant.

2. Specific behaviors are clearly stated.

3. The value, or payoff, to students who are doing a task well is highlighted.

4. Students' prior accomplishments are related to their current accomplishments.

5. Youngsters' actions and choices are credited as key elements in their achievements.

Positive feedback is less likely to increase motivation in the following circumstances (Brophy, 1981; Deci et al., 1996):

1. Positive feedback is framed as a comparison to others.

2. Feedback focuses on ability, independent of effort.

3. Feedback highlights external consequences, as in the case of complimenting youngsters for doing what the teacher asks or offering certain payoffs, such as winning a prize.

Ways Teachers' Attitudes and Values Affect Students' Motivation

There is a strong, positive association between students' willingness to ask for help and their motivation (Ryan et al., 1994). Students' willingness to seek help is strongly affected by teachers' attitudes and behavior. When teachers communicate, for example, that respecting and helping peers are important values, youngsters are more likely to feel safe and comfortable, less anxious about the possibility of making a mistake or looking foolish, and more likely to ask for help (Ryan et al., 2001). Similarly, students are more likely to seek help when teachers create opportunities for questions to be asked and respond to questions with warmth and the offer of support. Help seeking is also enhanced when teachers stress values such as the importance of understanding the schoolwork, relative improvement, and the intrinsic benefits of learning. On the other hand, students are less likely to seek help when teachers emphasize the importance of high grades or correct answers. When teachers highlight the importance of correct answers, youngsters are more likely to anticipate that they will be criticized through a public display of their relative lack of knowledge; thus they avoid asking for help (Ryan et al., 2001).

Teachers often possess different expectations for low-achieving students than they do for high-achieving students, and, as a result, again often discourage help seeking (Good, 1981). For example, teachers tend to call on low-achieving students less often than on high-achieving students, wait less time for them to respond, give them answers rather than guide them toward an alternative answer when they respond incorrectly, and praise them less frequently. Especially for low-achieving students who tend to expect failure, teachers need to reward students' attempts to ask for help and attach a positive meaning to the behavior. For example, help seeking can be praised as an attempt at self-reliance, as a demonstration of a desire to learn, and as initiative taking.

SUMMARY

Students who have repeatedly failed at school are often unmotivated. They tend to deny or minimize any positive purposes for exerting effort in order to learn. When at school, they tend to be disengaged, avoid academic challenges, expect to fail, and give up when the work is even somewhat frustrating. They often attribute their school failure to stable, internal perceived deficiencies—such as low intelligence—feel little control over school outcomes, and believe that there is little they can do to improve. Important contributors to their lack of motivation include difficulty in developing clear goals and standards for success, regulating attention and mood, employing effective study skills, and asking for help. At times, parents and teachers amplify students' lack of motivation by failing to appreciate the anxiety, hopelessness, and helplessness that underlie their lack of effort and by making demands to perform schoolwork in a harsh and controlling manner.

Teachers and caregivers can have a powerful influence on students' willingness to exert effort, degree of engagement, and tolerance for failure. Students are more motivated when the significant adults in their life are warm, provide support and constructive feedback, and convey the belief that they can be successful. Students are also more motivated when success is measured by the degree of effort demonstrated and the personal progress made, mistakes are viewed as an expected and acceptable aspect of learning, choice and accountability are encouraged, and help seeking is promoted.

Pregroup Student Assessment Outline

PREGROUP STUDENT ASSESSMENT OUTLINE

Student _____ Date _____

Assessor _____

Review of School Records

1. What type of special educational services has the youngster received, if any?

2. Are formal diagnoses present that are associated with chronic school difficulties, such as mild mental retardation, a specific learning disability, or an attention deficit disorder?

3. Is there evidence of significantly below grade level performance in one or more academic areas for at least one year? What explanations have been suggested for the deficient performance?

4. Are there comments about effort, attitude, and behavior that help define the nature of the youngster's motivation (e.g., has poor attendance, acts like a class clown)?

5. Are emotional problems and/or family stressors noted that are likely to be interfering with academic motivation?

From *Enhancing Academic Motivation: An Intervention Program for Young Adolescents.*
Copyright © 2006 by Norman Brier. Research Press (800-519-2707; www.researchpress.com)

(page 1 of 2)

Student Interview

1. How well do you do at your schoolwork compared to kids in your class? How well do you do compared to your siblings?

2. If you do less well, what do you think is the reason?

3. On a scale of 1 to 10, how much effort do you exert to do well at school overall? Are there some areas where you do work hard? Are there some areas where you hardly work at all? If you work harder in some areas than others, what do you think is the reason?

4. Do you expect to do badly at schoolwork?

5. Are there times when you feel scared, sad, angry, embarrassed and/or ashamed because you are unable to do your schoolwork as well as others?

6. Do you give up easily or not try to do your schoolwork if you find the work difficult?

7. Who encourages you to do your best at schoolwork?

Academic Motivation Screen

ACADEMIC MOTIVATION SCREEN

Student _____ Date of screen _____

Date of birth _____ Screener _____

Circle the number in the column that best describes how you acted and felt about your schoolwork **this past week.** Tell whether you felt or acted in the way described **never, some of the time, a lot of the time,** or **all or almost all the time**. Be sure to circle the number that is under the column heading that fits your answer.

Questions

When you were doing your schoolwork this past week, as best you can tell, did you:	Never	Some of the time	A lot of the time	All or almost all the time
1. try your best to finish your schoolwork?	0	1	2	3
2. worry that others would make fun of how you were doing?	3	2	1	0
3. pay attention?	0	1	2	3
4. ask for help when you needed it?	0	1	2	3
5. care how well you did?	0	1	2	3
6. feel sad because you thought you would do badly?	3	2	1	0
7. give up when you got "stuck"?	3	2	1	0
8. fight "discouraging" thoughts?	0	1	2	3
9. keep track of what you completed?	0	1	2	3
10. plan ahead of time what you needed to do?	0	1	2	3
11. worry that you were not doing as well as other students?	3	2	1	0
12. notice that you were making progress?				
13. put off doing your schoolwork?	3	2	1	0
14. set a goal that you thought you could accomplish if you tried?	0	1	2	3
15. figure out a way to be less nervous while doing the work?	0	1	2	3

SUBTOTALS ____ + ____ + ____ + ____

TOTAL SCORE ____

Session Handouts

Name _____ **Date** _____

In each of the situations listed below, first describe the activities that you like to do most; then, for each activity, tell if you try to do your best, and what things happen to make you try harder or give up.

1. When you are by yourself: _____

    _____

    _____

2. When you are with friends: _____

    _____

    _____

3. When you are with your family: _____

    _____

    _____

4. When you are at school: _____

    _____

    _____

5. During the summer: _____

    _____

6. During the winter: _____

    _____

    _____

Name _____ Date _____

1. Using the effort thermometer below, place an X on the spot that best indicates your overall effort for today.

0	10	20	30	40	50	60	70	80	90	100

2. Did you have trouble today trying your hardest?   ❏Yes   ❏ No

   If you answered yes, complete questions a–g. If you answered no, go on to question 3.

   a. What type of schoolwork were you doing when you had trouble trying your hardest?

   ❏ Class work
   ❏ Getting extra help
   ❏ Taking a test
   ❏ Homework
   Other _____

   b. What was going on at that time:

   ❏ Somebody teased me.
   ❏ I couldn't do the work.
   ❏ I got embarrassed.
   ❏ The teacher criticized me.
   ❏ I felt everyone was watching how I did.
   ❏ I did something wrong.
   ❏ I got confused.
   ❏ Other _____

   c. What did you feel?

	Not at all	A little bit	A lot
Sad	0	1	2
Scared	0	1	2
Mad	0	1	2
Happy	0	1	2
Frustrated	0	1	2

    d. What did you think?

      ❏ I was stupid.   ❏ I can do this.

      ❏ The work was stupid.   ❏ I am going to try.

      ❏ I hate school.

      ❏ Other _____

    e. What did you do?

      ❏ Tried   ❏ Walked out

      ❏ Acted silly   ❏ Got sad

      ❏ Asked for help   ❏ Got mad

      ❏ Gave up

      ❏ Other _____

    f. How do you think you handled this situation?

1	2	3	4	5
Poorly	Not so well	OK	Well	Great

    g. What could you do differently next time?

      ❏ Try harder

      ❏ Ask for help

      ❏ Ask permission to leave and come back when feeling better

      ❏ Other _____

3. Did you try to do schoolwork today even if you were scared that you would not do OK?

   ❏ Yes   ❏ No   ❏ Didn't come up

4. Did you judge how you did today according to how much progress you made?

   ❏ Yes   ❏ No   ❏ Didn't come up

5. Did you ask for help today if you were stuck?

   ❏ Yes   ❏ No   ❏ Didn't come up

Homework

_____

_____

_____

_____

_____

_____

_____

_____

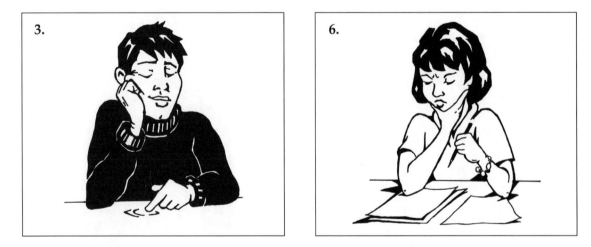

Estimating Your Level of School Stress

Name _____ **Date** _____

Read each statement, and considering how you felt this past week, answer *yes* if the statement is **True,** and *no* if the statement is **False.**

1. I worried a lot about how I was doing at school. ❏ Yes ❏ No

2. I couldn't concentrate when I tried to do my schoolwork. ❏ Yes ❏ No

3. I couldn't sleep because I was worried about school. ❏ Yes ❏ No

4. My head and/or stomach hurt when I was doing schoolwork. ❏ Yes ❏ No

5. I felt "jittery" when I was doing schoolwork. ❏ Yes ❏ No

6. I felt my heart "race" when I was doing schoolwork. ❏ Yes ❏ No

7. I had to check and double-check my schoolwork. ❏ Yes ❏ No

8. I worried that something bad was going to happen if I didn't do well. ❏ Yes ❏ No

Name _____ **Date** _____

Draw lines from the negative-thinking kid to the positive-thinking kid.

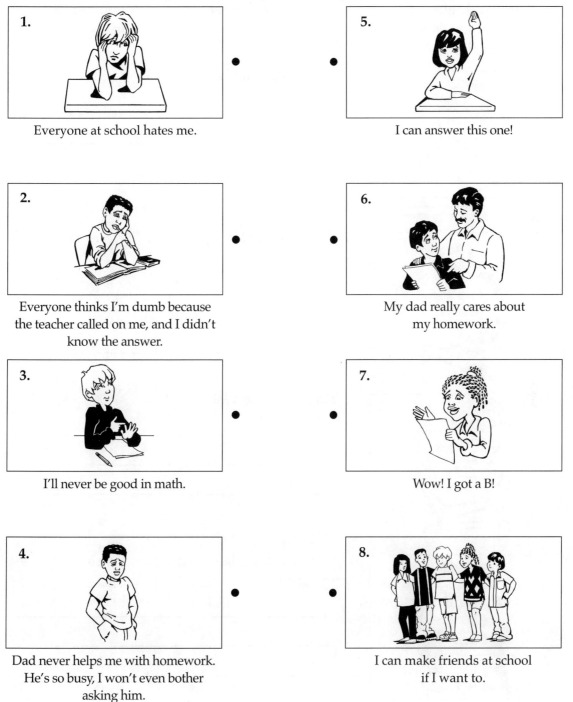

1.

Everyone at school hates me.

2.

Everyone thinks I'm dumb because the teacher called on me, and I didn't know the answer.

3.

I'll never be good in math.

4.

Dad never helps me with homework. He's so busy, I won't even bother asking him.

5.

I can answer this one!

6.

My dad really cares about my homework.

7.

Wow! I got a B!

8.

I can make friends at school if I want to.

Name _____ **Date** _____

The things people say to themselves sometimes make them act in a certain way, either good or bad. Pretend that you have a special power that allows you to read these students' minds. What might you suggest they say to themselves instead to help them behave better?

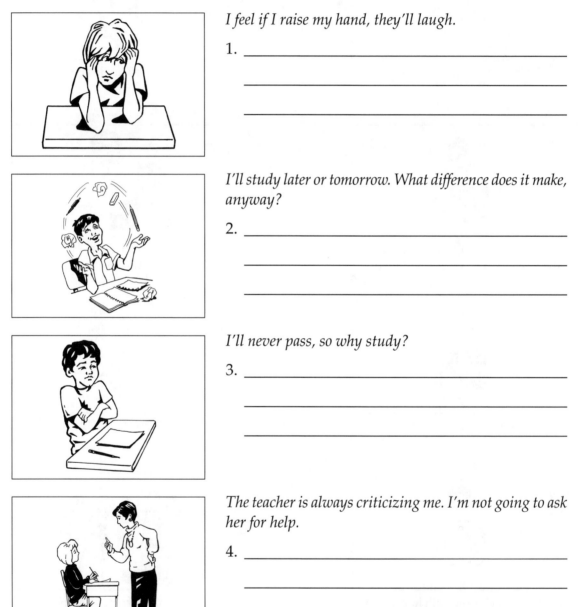

I feel if I raise my hand, they'll laugh.

1. _____

   _____

   _____

I'll study later or tomorrow. What difference does it make, anyway?

2. _____

   _____

   _____

I'll never pass, so why study?

3. _____

   _____

   _____

The teacher is always criticizing me. I'm not going to ask her for help.

4. _____

   _____

   _____

Step 1: Identify the problem.

Step 2: Think of all the alternatives.

Step 3: Consider the consequences of each alternative.

Step 4: Choose the best alternative and try it.

Step 5: Evaluate your choice.

Name _____ Date _____

What are your anxiety signals? See if you can identify which of these signals are present when you are upset.

FEELINGS

❏ Confused, overwhelmed   ❏ Uncomfortable, ill at ease

❏ Fearful, nervous, tense   ❏ Down in the dumps, tired

❏ Irritable

BEHAVIORS

❏ Move around a lot   ❏ Sleep too much or too little

❏ Easily startled   ❏ Forget things

❏ Eat too much or too little   ❏ Withdraw

BODY REACTIONS

❏ Upset stomach   ❏ Feel dizzy

❏ Heart pounds   ❏ Hands feel damp

❏ Muscles get tense   ❏ Clench jaw

❏ Breathe rapidly   ❏ Feel weak

❏ Feel "trembly"   ❏ Headaches

❏ Sweat   ❏ Feel hot or cold

❏ Get rashes   ❏ Throat feels tight

Name _____ **Date** _____

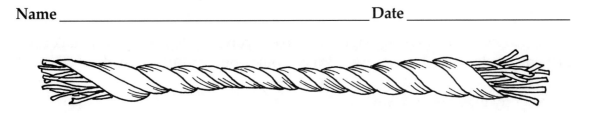

Imagine yourself as a tightly stretched rope. Check the phrases that fit how you feel like this rope.

❏ tight
❏ ready to snap
❏ tense
❏ none of the above

Now, pick a relaxation exercise and see if you can relax your muscles and loosen the rope. Again, check the phrases that now fit how you feel like this rope.

❏ tight
❏ ready to snap
❏ tense
❏ none of the above

What relaxation technique did you use?

_____

_____

Name _____ **Date** _____

Some people say that when you have worries, you have to learn how to talk back to them to help make them go away. What would you "say" to each of these worries?

1. Nobody likes you anyway.

   _____

   _____

2. You are really stupid when it comes to math.

   _____

   _____

3. You are going to be teased.

   _____

   _____

4. Go ahead—give up.

   _____

   _____

5. Don't raise your hand. The teacher won't like your answer anyway.

   _____

   _____

6. Everyone thinks that you are going to do badly at school.

   _____

   _____

Combating Worries Log

Name _____

Fill out this chart whenever you get worried. It's OK if you don't remember to write your thoughts down right away when you're worried, but try to fill the form out the same day.

Date	Event (What happened to make you worried?)	Coping self-statements (What did you say to yourself to cope and reduce your worries?)	Plan of action (What did you do to solve the problem? Did you try to relax or ask for help?)	Rating of effectiveness (1—didn't work to 10—worked very well)

From *Enhancing Academic Motivation: An Intervention Program for Young Adolescents*. Copyright © 2006 by Norman Brier. Research Press (800-519-2707; www.researchpress.com)

Name _____ **Date** _____

1. We all need help sometimes at school. Tell about a time at school this past week when you did need help.

   _____

   _____

   _____

2. Was it hard for you to ask for help? If so, why?

   _____

   _____

   _____

3. Whom did you ask for help?

   _____

   _____

   _____

4. How did you ask? (What did you say and do?)

   _____

   _____

   _____

5. Did you pick the right time to ask?

   _____

   _____

   _____

6. Afterwards, were you glad you asked for help or sorry that you did?

   _____

   _____

   _____

When I Want to Avoid Schoolwork Log

Fill out this log whenever you feel you want to avoid schoolwork. It's OK if you don't remember to write your thoughts down right away, but try to fill the form out the same day.

Date	Event (What happened to make you want to avoid your work?)	How did your body feel? (Describe breathing, muscles tensing, heart rate, etc.)	What were your thoughts? (What did you say to yourself?)	What did you do? (What actions did you take?)

1. Organize your study space to reduce distractions.

2. Try to do your work when you are calm and rested.

3. Create a routine for doing your schoolwork. Do the same things in the same order as much as possible.

4. Look at the assignment or, if it was presented orally, remember the words. Make a mental picture of what you have to do and decide on the order in which you need to do it.

5. Check regularly to make sure you are on task.

6. If you begin to feel tense or frustrated, use a relaxation technique.

7. Afterwards, evaluate how well you have paid attention. Compliment yourself on any progress that you have made, and see if there is anything you might do differently next time to improve your concentration.

Raymond's Disorganized Desk

Name _____ **Date** _____

Raymond had a very important homework assignment. His teacher said that it had to be neat or he would get a bad grade. Raymond really wanted to be more organized, but his desk was pretty messy. Can you help him out? Circle all the things on Raymond's desk that shouldn't be there.

From *Enhancing Academic Motivation: An Intervention Program for Young Adolescents.*
Copyright © 2006 by Norman Brier. Research Press (800-519-2707; www.researchpress.com)

Where I Do My Schoolwork

Name _____ **Date** _____

Think about where you do your schoolwork and answer **yes** or **no** to each of the following questions.

The place where I do my schoolwork . . .	Yes	No
1. is quiet.	❏	❏
2. has no distractions (for example, no TV, no brother playing next to where I sit).	❏	❏
3. has enough light.	❏	❏
4. has a comfortable chair.	❏	❏
5. has all the work materials I need close at hand.	❏	❏
6. has a desk or table large enough to work at comfortably.	❏	❏
7. is private.	❏	❏
8. is neat.	❏	❏

My Real Study Space

Name _____ **Date** _____

Show where your study space is in your home, and draw the furniture, tools, and materials you really have there.

From *Enhancing Academic Motivation: An Intervention Program for Young Adolescents.*
Copyright © 2006 by Norman Brier. Research Press (800-519-2707; www.researchpress.com)

Name _____ **Date** _____

Now draw your ideal study space. Be sure to show everything you would like to have in it.

Assignment Sheet

Name _____ **Date** _____

❏ Take your assignment sheet to every class.

❏ Write down each assignment as soon as you hear it.

❏ Look over your assignment sheet at the end of the school day before you leave school so you know which books and materials you need to take home.

❏ Read your assignment sheet when you get ready to do your homework so you know exactly what you have to do.

❏ After you complete an assignment, check "Completed!"

Class/subject _____ Today's date _____

Assignment _____

Due date _____ # of days till due _____ ❏ Completed!

Class/subject _____ Today's date _____

Assignment _____

Due date _____ # of days till due _____ ❏ Completed!

Class/subject _____ Today's date _____

Assignment _____

Due date _____ # of days till due _____ ❏ Completed!

Class/subject _____ Today's date _____

Assignment _____

Due date _____ # of days till due _____ ❏ Completed!

Class/subject _____ Today's date _____

Assignment _____

Due date _____ # of days till due _____ ❏ Completed!

Assignment Planner

Name _____ **Date** _____

Fill in the chart below with the tasks you need to do, the order in which you will complete them, and the amount of time you think you'll need to do each task. After you complete each task, check "Completed."

Assignment

_____

_____

Order you will do tasks	Component tasks	Estimate # of minutes or hours to complete	Actual # of minutes or hours needed to complete	Completed ✓
1				❏
2				❏
3				❏
4				❏
5				❏
6				❏
7				❏
8				❏
9				❏
10				❏

Name _____ **Date** _____

	YES	NO
1. Did I prepare (make a plan)?	❏	❏
2. Did I prioritize?	❏	❏
3. Did I make a schedule?	❏	❏
4. When carrying out my plan, did I ask for help when I needed it?	❏	❏
5. Was I organized?	❏	❏
6. Did I check to make sure that I did all the work and that it was done correctly?	❏	❏

1. To try your best to learn at school, you need to believe that there is a benefit to you that you consider important.

2. The best way to tell if you are motivated is by the amount of effort that you put forth (not by the grades you get).

3. School success is best measured by your personal progress, not by whether you are doing better or worse than other students.

4. If you try your best and see that you are making progress, you are likely to experience the positive feelings of pride and mastery.

5. Even if you are not as good as other students at a school task, effort and assistance from a teacher are often sufficient to help you improve.

6. Noticing the things that you do, or stop doing, that help you make progress is important in order to feel proud of your efforts.

7. Feedback is almost always necessary in order to correct errors and make progress. Feedback is only helpful, however, if you hear the feedback accurately.

8. You need to be sure that you are hearing feedback accurately when you are upset and, likewise, be sure at these times that your explanations for why you may not have done well fits the facts.

9. If you feel helpless and hopeless, set a short-term goal that is fair—that is, a goal that you can achieve if you try hard. Pay special attention to how your effort affects the amount of progress that you make. Be sure to take credit for any progress you earn by your effort.

10. If you feel discouraged, try to challenge your "down thoughts," and problem solve—for example, try to find someone who can show you a new strategy.

11. Anxious feelings interfere with motivation. Try to be aware of your anxiety signals and, once you identify them, use a relaxation technique, self-talk, and/or problem solving to reduce the anxiety that you are feeling.

12. Often when someone feels anxious about how well they can do in carrying out a school task, they try to avoid doing it. If you have the urge to avoid schoolwork, try to figure out what you are afraid of, set a reasonable goal, have courage, and, try, focusing on how much effort you are putting out. Compliment yourself on your courage. It is hard to try in the presence of anxiety.

13. Ask for help, especially when you have been trying and are still unsure how to do the work.

14. You need to pay attention in order to improve. It is easier to pay attention if you organize your study space and eliminate potential distractions. Create a routine, and regularly check to see if you are on track.

Certificate of Achievement

_____
Student

has been awarded this certificate for effort
in completing academic motivation training

_____
Leader signature

_____
Date

APPENDIX D

Parent Involvement

Parents and other caregivers need to support and encourage their youngsters' desire and ability to expend effort on school-work. The most important things they can do to help include the following:

✦ Focus on effort and personal progress rather than grades or comparisons with others

✦ Elicit their youngster's feelings about his or her performance

✦ Allow the youngster some control over when and how school-work is carried out

✦ Provide positive feedback and suggestions as to what might be done differently, rather than focusing on the negative and giving criticism

✦ Help the youngster establish and maintain an effective study place

PARENT MATERIALS

In working toward the goal of improved academic motivation in their children, parents need to become aware of and, to the extent possible, apply the information in the knowledge base to their own child's situations. A sample letter to parents and guardians, briefly describing the intervention, asking their permission, and inviting their questions, is provided on page 145. Also included is a summary of the knowledge base on academic motivation, written especially for parents. This summary, titled "How Parents and Caregivers Influence Academic Motivation," appears on pages 146–149. Session leaders may feel free to photocopy and adapt these materials as needed.

PARENT CONTACT

To let parents know about the intervention and request their permission, you may mail a copy of the letter and summary to parents. You may also give students these materials at the recommended one-on-one meeting or at the first session of the intervention. Students can then take these materials home and share them with their parents.

Ideally, parents will be able to participate in a workshop to discuss the information in the knowledge base and apply it to their own child's situation. A parent workshop can be structured for a single meeting or broken into as many meetings as time permits. Having at least two meetings is recommended. The first session will give parents the opportunity to process the knowledge base, discuss some of the motivation challenges their own youngsters face, and determine which ideas they would like to try. In the second meeting, parents can describe what happened when they tried out the ideas. The following general questions are helpful in asking parents about their experiences:

What happened in the situation?

How easy or difficult was it to carry out the idea?

How well or poorly did the attempt go?

Workshop members may comment on the attempt, praise what they think went well, and offer alternative ways of carrying out the idea. They may also propose other ideas from the knowledge base that might be helpful.

SAMPLE PARENT/GUARDIAN LETTER

Dear Parent or Guardian:

Staying motivated to do schoolwork is a problem for many students. Some, especially students with a history of school failure, are especially likely to anticipate failure and feel frustrated when doing schoolwork.

Your child is invited to participate in an intervention designed to help increase students' ability to stay motivated to do the best they can on their schoolwork. The sessions your child will attend will address the attitudes and behaviors associated with improved academic motivation. Sessions will be held from _____ to _____ .

The specific goals of the intervention are as follows:

- ✦ To increase your child's willingness to approach learning tasks
- ✦ To bring about a higher level of engagement while learning
- ✦ To encourage your child to demonstrate a higher level of effort
- ✦ To help your child persist at learning tasks, even in the face of frustration

Please sign and return the bottom portion of this letter if you grant permission for your child to participate in this intervention. If you have questions, please feel free to contact me at _____ .

Sincerely,
Session Leader

I grant permission for my child, _____ ,
to participate in academic motivation sessions as part of an intervention to help students do the best they can on their schoolwork.

_____   _____
Parent/guardian signature   *Date*

From *Enhancing Academic Motivation: An Intervention Program for Young Adolescents.*
Copyright © 2006 by Norman Brier. Research Press (800-519-2707; www.researchpress.com)

How Parents and Caregivers Influence Academic Motivation

Parents and caregivers can help their youngsters stay motivated and do well in their schoolwork. The main way that parents can contribute is by becoming actively involved in their youngsters' school experiences and by exhibiting a positive attitude toward their school accomplishments. Here are some common questions parents ask. The answers come from the studies of academic motivation that researchers have conducted.

1. How can I tell if my child is motivated?

Children are highly motivated if they want to learn, attempt learning tasks, stay engaged after beginning work, and exert a high degree of effort and persistence while learning, even if frustrated or anxious. In addition, they are highly motivated if they think doing their best at school is important, believe they can do the work well, and employ effective strategies to increase their chances of being successful.

2. How can I help my child feel that schoolwork matters?

The more your child sees that doing schoolwork is valuable, desirable, or attractive—and can think of a personal goal or purpose for doing the work—the more your child is likely to want to try his or her best. It is especially important that your youngster see himself or herself as the main beneficiary of doing well at school—for example, wants to do well to experience pride when performing school tasks. Your child's motivation is likely to be relatively low if he or she tries only to please you or to avoid getting punished.

3. Does the way I judge school success affect my child's motivation?

Your youngster is more likely to be motivated if you judge school success by the amount and duration of your youngster's effort and

(page 1 of 5)

by the degree of progress or improvement he or she makes. Your youngster is likely to be less motivated if you judge school success by your youngster's ability to outperform others, achieve a particular grade, or receive positive judgments from others. Youngsters who focus on effort, improvement, and personal progress generally are more willing to take on academic challenges, continue to try even when faced with obstacles, and think less about the possibility of failure and embarrassment. Youngsters who focus on outperforming others and on getting favorable judgments from others are more likely to feel embarrassed and ashamed. In addition, when faced with a difficult academic task, they are more likely to feel helpless and frustrated, and as a result, give up. Therefore, it is helpful to tell your youngster clearly what you consider success in doing schoolwork and to regularly compliment effort and personal progress.

4. How important is it for my child to believe that he or she is capable of doing schoolwork?

Youngsters generally answer the question "Can I do the work?" on the basis of their past history of school successes and failures. This information is then used to develop expectations, or predictions, about the likelihood of future school success. When youngsters feel capable of doing their schoolwork, they are more likely to be motivated and more likely to see their schoolwork as having value. It is important periodically to ask your youngster how he or she feels with regard to the ability to do schoolwork, offer assistance, and discuss differences between your youngster's perceptions of his or her capabilities and your perceptions. Your child's beliefs about past school successes and failures are not based only on the objective results of school performance. How your youngster *interprets* these facts is also extremely important. For example, if your youngster has generally received passing grades but has been in a school with very high achievers, he or she may have gotten lower grades than other youngsters and feel discouraged and incapable. Encouraging your youngster to say how he or she feels about school performance is important and provides an opportunity for you to encourage your youngster to focus less on comparisons and more on personal progress. Having your youngster express feelings and focus on effort and personal progress are especially important when there is a poor match between your youngster's capabilities and the academic demands and support he or she is receiving. Your youngster has less control over attaining a "good" grade in these circumstances.

5. What effects do my attitudes about the value of schoolwork have on my child's motivation?

Your youngster's motivation is strongly affected by your attitudes and values toward school and schoolwork. The more importance you attach to schoolwork, the more likely your youngster will put forth effort and display interest in schoolwork. Youngsters usually judge the importance of schoolwork to their parents by their parents' knowledge about what they are doing in school and their parents' interest in school activities. In addition, students' motivation is likely to be higher the more they believe that their parents notice their efforts and any distress they may have when doing schoolwork. Interestingly, when youngsters feel that parents are concerned about their schoolwork, they are more likely to do their schoolwork on their own. Parent involvement with school activities also raises youngsters' motivation by making it more likely that youngsters will get extra help, when needed. As a result, they will feel less frustrated and defeated. Youngsters are more likely to ask for help with schoolwork—and are better able to cope when they experience academic failure—if parents show an interest in giving them the support they need.

6. How important is feedback to motivation?

How you evaluate and correct your youngster's schoolwork strongly affects his or her motivation. Your youngster's motivation is likely to be higher the more you maintain a positive focus—that is, when you highlight what your youngster is doing right and point out what he or she might do differently to improve. Your youngster's motivation is likely to be lower the more you focus on what he or she is doing wrong and continually point out errors. It is particularly helpful to praise positive outcomes that your youngster can achieve if he or she tries. These outcomes include displaying effort, persevering, and seeking help. On the other hand, your youngster's motivation is likely to be lower when you focus on things that your youngster cannot directly control, such as grades and academic standing in relation to others. In addition, praise is most likely to increase motivation if it is given as close in time as possible to a positive behavior; includes the details that led to the praise (so your youngster is clear about what he or she did right and believes you); highlights your youngster's role in the achievement (so your youngster can see how his or her actions have contributed to the positive outcome and knows how to reproduce the outcome); and emphasizes the benefits of the positive behavior to your youngster rather than to you (for instance, "You really worked hard studying for that math test. Now you know you can do this stuff when you try" rather than "I'm glad you did what I told you to do").

7. Is there a best way to tell my child to do schoolwork?

Your youngster is likely to be more motivated if you first invite him or her to express feelings about what is a reasonable expectation for school success and incorporate these views, if possible, when discussing what you expect in terms of school behavior. Your youngster is less likely to be motivated, on the one hand, if you use a controlling style and do not allow him or her any input in the discussion and, on the other hand, if you are overly permissive and do not define expectations, instead allowing the youngster to do whatever he or she wants. By defining clear expectations with your child's participation, you increase the chance that your child will feel more control over the outcome of schoolwork and as a result, will feel increased pride in achievement. Youngsters can, for example, be allowed input into such choices as when to begin schoolwork, which task they will start with, and how long they will work before taking a break.

8. Is it important to plan where my child will do schoolwork?

Your youngster's motivation is affected by where he or she does his or her schoolwork. Motivation is likely to be higher when you collaborate with your youngster and decide together what constitutes the best study space available. For example, together you can look for the place in the house that is quietest and most free of distractions. Because motivation is also affected by how neat and organized the study space is, you can also help increase and maintain your youngster's motivation by first providing assistance to organize the study space and make sure that your youngster has the necessary supplies and that these supplies are easily accessible. Finally, you can help ensure that the study space stays neat and organized by periodically doing a "checkup" and, as needed, encouraging cleanup and reorganization.

References

Ames, C., & Archer, J. (1988). Achievement goals in the classroom: Students' learning strategies and motivational processes. *Journal of Educational Psychology, 80,* 60–67.

Bandura, A. (1994). *Self-efficacy: The exercise of control.* New York: Freeman.

Berndt, T. J., Laychak, A. E., & Pack, K. (1990). Friends' influence on adolescents' academic achievement motivation: An experimental study. *Journal of Educational Psychology, 82,* 664–670.

Borkowski, J. G., & Thorpe, P. K. (1994). Self-regulation and motivation: A life-span perspective on underachievement. In D. H. Schunk & B. J. Zimmerman (Eds.), *Self-regulation of learning and performance.* Hillsdale, NJ: Erlbaum.

Brophy, J. (1981). Teacher praise: A functional analysis. *Review of Educational Research, 51*(1), 5–32.

Brophy, J. (1987). Socializing students' motivation to learn. In M. L. Maehr & D. A. Keliber (Eds.), *Advances in motivation and achievement* (Vol. 5). Greenwich, CT: JAI Press.

Carr, M., Borkowski, J. G., & Maxwell, S. E. (1991). Motivational components of underachievement. *Developmental Psychology, 27,* 108–118.

Covington, M. V. (1992). Making the grade: *A self-worth perspective on motivation and school reform.* New York: Cambridge University Press.

Csikszentmihalyi, M. (1988). The flow experience and its significance for human psychology. In M. Csikszentmihalyi & J. S. Csikszentmihalyi (Eds.), *Optimal experience* (pp. 15–35). Cambridge MA: Cambridge University Press.

deCharms, R. (1968). *Personal causation: The internal affective determinants of behavior.* New York: Academic Press.

Deci, E. L., Ryan, R. M., & Williams, G. C. (1996). Need satisfaction and the self-regulation of learning. *Learning and Individual Differences, 8,* 165–183.

Dunkin, M., & Biddle, B. (1974). *The study of teaching.* New York: Holt, Rinehart and Winston.

Dweck, C. S., & Elliot, E. S. (1983). Achievement motivation. In P. H. Mussen (Ed.), *Handbook of child psychology* (3rd ed.; Vol. 4., pp. 643–691). New York: Wiley.

Dweck, C. S., & Goetz, T. E. (1978). Attributions and learned helplessness. In J. H. Harvey, W. Ackes, & R. F. Kidd (Eds.), *New directions in attribution research* (Vol. 2). Hillsdale, NJ: Erlbaum.

Eccles, J. S., Buchanan, C. M., Fuligni, A., Midgley, C. M., & Yee, D. (1991). Control and autonomy: Individuation revisited in early adolescence. *Journal of Social Issues, 47,* 53–68.

Eccles, J. S., Wigfield, A., & Schiefele, V. (1998). Motivation to succeed. In W. Damon & N. Eisenberg (Eds.), *Handbook of Child Psychology: Vol. 3. Social, emotional, and personality development* (5th ed., pp. 1017–1095). Hoboken, NJ: Wiley.

Eccles-Parsons, J., Adler, T. F., Futterman, R., Goff, S. B., Kaczala, C. M., Meece, J. L., & Midgley, C. (1983). Expectancies, values, and academic behaviors. In J. T. Spence (Ed.), *Achievement and achievement motivation* (pp. 75–146). San Francisco: Freeman.

Gall, M. D., Gall, J. P., Jacobson, D. R., & Bullock, T. L. (1990). *Tools for learning: A guide to teaching study skills.* Alexandria, VA: Association for Supervision and Curriculum Development.

Garcia, T. (1996). Self-regulation: An introduction. *Learning and Individual Differences, 8,* 161–163.

Good, T. (1981). Teacher expectations and student perceptions: A decade of research. *Journal of Educational Psychology, 38,* 415–423.

Good, T. (1983). Classroom research: A decade of progress. *Educational Psychologist, 18*(3), 127–144.

Graham, S. (1990). Communicating low ability in the classroom: Bad things good teachers sometimes do. In S. Graham & V. S. Folkes (Eds.), *Attribution theory: Applications to achievement, mental health, and interpersonal conflict* (pp. 17–36). Hillsdale, NJ: Erlbaum.

Grolnick, W. S., & Ryan, R. M. (1989). Parent styles associated with children's self-regulation and competence in school. *Journal of Educational Psychology, 81,* 143–154.

Harter, S. (1981). A new self-report scale of intrinsic versus extrinsic orientation in the classroom: Motivational and informational components. *Developmental Psychology, 17,* 300–312.

Kirk, S. A., & Chalfant, J. C. (1984). *Academic and developmental learning disabilities.* Columbus, OH: Love Publishing.

Linnenbrink, E. A., & Pintrich, P. R. (2002). Motivation as an enabler of academic success. *School Psychology Review, 31,* 313–327.

MacIver, D. J., Reuman, D. A., & Main, S. R. (1995). Social structuring of the school: Studying what is, illuminating what could be. *Annual Review of Psychology, 46,* 375–400.

Maehr, M. L., & Midgley, C. (1996). *Transforming school culture.* Boulder: Westview Press.

Moos, R. H. (1979). *Evaluating educational environment.* San Francisco: Jossey-Bass.

Nicholls, J. G. (1979). Quality and equality in intellectual development: The role of motivation in education. *American Psychologist, 34,* 1071–1084.

Nicholls, J. G., Patashnick, M., & Mettetal, G. (1986). Conceptions of ability and intelligence. *Child Development, 57,* 636–645.

Pintrich, P. R., & Schunk, D. H. (2002). *Motivation in education: Theory, research, and applications* (2nd ed.). Upper Saddle River, NJ: Prentice Hall.

Roeser, R. W., Midgley, C., & Urdan, T. (1996). Perceptions of the school environment and early adolescents' psychological and behavioral functioning in school: The mediating role of goals and belonging. *Journal of Educational Psychology, 88*(3), 408–422.

Rosenthal, R. (1973). The Pygmalion effect lives. *Psychology Today, 7*(4), 56–63.

Ryan, R. M., & Deci, E. L. (2000). Self-determination theory and the facilitation of intrinsic motivation, social development, and well-being. *American Psychologist, 55,* 68–78.

Ryan, R. M., Pintrich, P. R., & Midgley, C. (2001). Avoiding seeking help in the classroom: Who and why? *Educational Psychology Review, 13,* 93–114.

Ryan, R. M., Stiller, J., & Lynch, J. H. (1994). Representations of relationships to teachers, parents, and friends as predictors of academic motivation and self-esteem. *Journal of Early Adolescence, 14,* 226–249.

Schunk, D. H. (1983). Ability versus effort attributional feedback: Differential effects on self-efficacy and achievement. *Journal of Educational Psychology, 75,* 848–856.

Stipek, D. J. (1996). Motivation and instruction. In R. C. Calfree & D. C. Berliner (Eds.), *Handbook of educational psychology.* New York: Macmillan.

Urdan, T., & Midgley, C. (2001). Academic self-handicapping: What we know, what more there is to learn. *Educational Psychology Review, 13,* 115–138.

Weiner, B. (1986). *An attributional theory of motivation and emotion.* New York: Springer-Verlag.

Weiner, B., Graham, S., Stern, P., & Lawson, M. E. (1982). Using affective clues to infer causal thoughts. *Developmental Psychology, 18*(2), 278–286.

Zimmerman, B. J. (1989). A social cognitive view of self-regulated learning. *Journal of Educational Psychology, 81,* 329–339.

Zimmerman, B. J., Bonner, S., & Kovach, R. L. (1996). *Developing self-regulated learners: Beyond achievement to self-efficacy.* Washington, DC: American Psychological Association.

About the Author

Dr. Norman Brier received his doctoral degree in psychology from Yeshiva University. Currently, he is a clinical professor of pediatrics and psychiatry at Albert Einstein College of Medicine, Bronx, New York, where he directs an adolescent division focusing on youngsters with histories of chronic school failure. He is the author of many articles and chapters addressing the psychological and social difficulties of adolescents with learning and developmental disabilities. In addition, he maintains a private practice in Westchester County, New York.